CHATTAHOOCHEE TRAILS

CHATTAHOOCHEE TRAILS

A GUIDE TO THE TRAILS OF THE CHATTAHOOCHEE
RIVER NATIONAL RECREATION AREA

William J. Linkous III

Copyright © 2015 by William J. Linkous III.

Library of Congress Control Number: 2015918146
ISBN: Hardcover   978-1-5144-2269-4
        Softcover   978-1-5144-2270-0
        eBook   978-1-5144-2268-7

All rights reserved. No part of this book may be reproduced or transmitted in any form or by any means, electronic or mechanical, including photocopying, recording, or by any information storage and retrieval system, without permission in writing from the copyright owner.

Any people depicted in stock imagery provided by Thinkstock are models, and such images are being used for illustrative purposes only.
Certain stock imagery © Thinkstock.

Print information available on the last page.

Rev. date: 11/05/2015

To order additional copies of this book, contact:
Xlibris
1-888-795-4274
www.Xlibris.com
Orders@Xlibris.com
549957

CONTENTS

ACKNOWLEDGMENTS vii
INTRODUCTION ix

CHAPTER 1   Tips For Visiting The CRNRA 1
    Scope of this Book 1
    What to Do 2
        Hiking/Walking 3
        Trail Running 3
        Biking 4
        Boating 5
        Fishing 5
        Wildlife Observation 6
        Rock Climbing 8
        Picnicking 8
        Family Fun 9
        Viewing Wildflowers 9
    Seasons in the CRNRA 10
    Rules and More Rules (CRNRA Regulations) 11
    What to Bring 13
    Safety 15
    Conservation and Awareness 18

CHAPTER 2   The Paces Mill/West Palisades
                Unit - Creek Meets River 20
    Sidebar 1 Rottenwood Creek 32
    Sidebar 2 Rock Climbing 33

CHAPTER 3   The East Palisades Unit - Shoals And Much More 47
    Sidebar 1 Long Island Creek 57
    Sidebar 2 East Palisades from the North 58

CHAPTER 4 The Powers Island Unit - Small But Beautiful..................71

CHAPTER 5 The Cochran Shoals/Sope Creek Unit - Crowds
And Solitude.. 80
Sidebar 1 Trail Running..105
Sidebar 2 Sope Creek..106

CHAPTER 6 The Johnson's Ferry South Unit - Wildlife
Abounds Here..124
Sidebar 1 Columns Drive...127

CHAPTER 7 The Johnson's Ferry North Unit - Flowers
In The Spring 132
Sidebar 1 Toadshade Trillium..136

CHAPTER 8 The Gold Branch Unit - Bull Sluice Lake......................144

CHAPTER 9 The Vickery Creek Unit - History
And Roswell Area Trails 163
Sidebar 1 Roswell History..172

CHAPTER 10 The Island Ford Unit - Park Headquarters 179

INDEX 197

ACKNOWLEDGMENTS

Writing a book is a serious undertaking. Writing a book describing trails and natural features is especially difficult because it requires two steps rather than just one. A writer describing trails must first collect information by repeatedly visiting the natural area on which the book is written and then create the written volume based on the research undertaken. Fortunately, I have spent most of my life living near the Chattahoochee River National Recreation Area and playing within its borders. My research was done all throughout my life, making it easier to repeat for the purposes of this book. I was sometimes tempted to write detailed trail descriptions in the book simply from memory but, instead, made sure to hike each of the trails repeatedly for the purposes of this book.

Nonetheless, I would be quite remiss if I do not acknowledge the many people who have enjoyed the CRNRA with me and who have helped me with many elements of this book. Foremost among those who have accompanied me into the CRNRA are the members of my family. My sons, Will and Ryan, and my daughter, Kara, have spent many hours with me hiking trails in the CRNRA, not realizing that their father was conducting research for a book. My brother, Brian, hiked and ran with me on trails at the CRNRA. Each of them deserves many thanks for assisting me and for sharing the beauty of the CRNRA.

I would also like to thank Phil Hollman, with whom I have spent countless hours hiking, camping, fishing, climbing, and paddling. Phil accompanied me on many evening rock climbing trips into the CRNRA, teaching me how to rock climb there. Phil and I also paddled the cold water of the river and of Bull Sluice Lake in kayaks. In fact, my first experience in paddling a kayak was on Bull Sluice Lake with Phil. Others who accompanied me to the CRNRA and deserve my thanks include

Steve and Cynthia Lang, Teo Roncal, Faruk Tasdemir, Kristian Nielsen, and Eric Letbetter. Many thanks also go to the countless others who have accompanied me and rendered assistance in the research and production of this book.

I am happy to have shared the beauty of the CRNRA with many other friendly folks, and I hope that they have enjoyed it as much as I have.

INTRODUCTION

I hope you can enjoy a visit to the Chattahoochee River National Recreation Area soon! Many residents of the metropolitan Atlanta area are unaware that an incredibly beautiful spot for hiking, running, biking, paddling, climbing, and nature observation is literally minutes away from their home in our fair city. Having lived near the river and the Chattahoochee River National Recreation Area (CRNRA) for nearly all my life and having fully explored the area in all seasons, I must admit that I am at a loss for sufficient superlatives when describing this incredible place. The beauty in the CRNRA must be experienced often to be believed. Cooped up in offices and beset by traffic jams, Atlantans should rejoice that a treasure like the CRNRA is so close by. Go visit the area and hike the trails in the spring and fall, and you won't be disappointed.

In the CRNRA, I've seen many species of wildlife, such as a coyote, deer, beaver, hawk, owl, and heron. I've seen fields of wildflowers in spring and spent whole afternoons taking pictures of them. I've walked through and around interesting historical sites, such as ruins of mills, houses, and other buildings and old cemeteries. I've enjoyed the vivid green of huge trees sprouting leaves in the spring against an azure-blue sky, and I've marveled at the incredible hues of yellow, red, orange, and maroon as fall colors blanketed the hills around the river. In the summer, the trees provide cool shade from the sun as their leaves rustle in the breeze brought along by the water, and the winter fog from the river creeps through the area and gives it a quiet, secluded peace.

Although the CRNRA can be savored for its nature alone, there are many other reasons to take to the trails of the CRNRA. One of my favorite pursuits in the CRNRA is trail running. Many runners already know about the main fitness trail at Cochran Shoals, but how many know about the other wonderful trail-running opportunities to be found throughout the CRNRA? Many of the local cross-country teams, including those from local high schools and from Georgia State University, train in the CRNRA. There are trails to explore for all levels of runners and trails that challenge you to increase your trail-running stamina.

Would you prefer to ride a bike? The CRNRA's fitness trail at Cochran Shoals is open to bikes and provides a leisurely ride for anyone, including families. Cochran Shoals is also one terminus for a challenging mountain biking trail that leads through the woods to the area around Sope Creek, and the same trail has recently been upgraded to provide a long loop through the woods near the Cochran Shoals Unit. Road bikers also enjoy biking along Columns Drive, a flat road that parallels the river, accesses several of the CRNRA units, and leads to many beautiful homes. Although outside the scope of this book, the CRNRA units also include rock cliffs for rock climbing and numerous opportunities for paddling in the river.

Regardless of the method you choose to enjoy this incredible area, please take care of it. Don't leave trash, go off-trail, or violate rules or regulations. Don't frighten dogs and people by speeding on your bike. Clean up after your dog. Your care for this fragile area will benefit others and, ultimately, benefit you. Please read all posted regulations and follow them.

I hope that this book will enhance your enjoyment of the CRNRA by leading you to new experiences and by pointing out features that you might have missed without it. I intentionally included no maps in the book. Instead, I decided to include numerous photographs of the CRNRA. I'm hoping that these differences will create a more unique experience for readers of this guidebook. In writing the book, I decided that I would make the text of the book clear enough that readers could follow my descriptions without consulting maps. Also, I felt that using descriptions without maps would add to the challenge and enjoyment of finding your way through the CRNRA, particularly because CRNRA trails are so short that it is difficult to become truly lost. I hope that my strategy adds to the value of the book for readers and keeps them reading rather than just glancing at maps.

For those who feel most secure with map in hand, you can obtain full copies of most of the necessary maps at the CRNRA website.

In writing this book, I checked my route descriptions many times to make sure that they are accurate. Nonetheless, I can give no guarantee that they will always guide you in the correct direction. Trees fall across trails; streams wash out bridges, and the National Park Service reroutes its trails. There are many factors that can lead to inaccurate trail descriptions. In fact, as I write this, the National Park Service is changing the course of many trails in a couple of the major units covered by this book. I'll try to describe those changes for you. But make sure that you use good common sense and route finding at all times in the CRNRA.

Many Atlanta nature lovers bemoan the long drive to the mountains or the coast for a "nature fix." By purchasing this book, you will be opening a doorway into numerous areas that will more than satisfy your craving for nature and solitude. When you are hiking one of the trails in the CRNRA described in this book, take a moment to pause, look around, and imagine that you are in the mountains. I suspect that your surroundings will not give away your location near the heart of metropolitan Atlanta. I hope that your experience at the CRNRA is most enjoyable and satisfies your craving for the great outdoors!

Oh, and one more thing! If you would like to see (or purchase) photographs that I have taken in the Chattahoochee River National Recreation Area and other locales, please visit my photo website at www.BillLinkous.Zenfolio.com. Enjoy!

Snakes such as this one in the Cochran Shoals Unit are not uncommon in the CRNRA

Beautiful ground cover in the Johnson's Ferry North Unit

Catesby's Trillium

Chattahoochee River shoals

Sibley Pond in the Cochran Shoals/Sope Creek Unit can be beautiful in the spring.

Wild azalea can be found in the Cochran Shoals/Sope Creek Unit of the CRNRA in the spring.

Wildlife such as turtles can be found at Sibley Pond in the Cochran Shoals/Sope Creek Unit.

CHAPTER 1

TIPS FOR VISITING THE CRNRA

Before I begin to disclose the secret areas of the CRNRA, I will provide some tips that will increase the chances that you will greatly enjoy your visit to the CRNRA. These tips and thoughts will set you on the right path. As you read these tips, always keep in mind that trails can be dangerous. You are solely responsible for your own safety while using CRNRA trails. Make sure to take the necessary precautions to ensure that your outing is a fun experience rather than an epic.

Scope of this Book

In writing this book, I initially struggled to decide which areas and activities would be included. There is so much to do in the many CRNRA tracts of land extending north from metropolitan Atlanta toward the headwaters of the river that I found it difficult to include everything or exclude anything. In the end, I decided to include those areas from the CRNRA headquarters at the Island Ford Unit southward (downstream). The primary benefit of limiting the scope of this book to include only the Island Ford Unit and those areas downstream is that these areas are more frequented, are closer to Atlanta, and contain many interesting trails. Perhaps I will detail the trails in the areas upstream of the Island Ford Unit in a sequel. But for the time being, this book should provide the reader with many opportunities for fun.

I also decided to limit the primary goal of this book to descriptions of the CRNRA trails. Although there are many wonderful activities that one can enjoy at the CRNRA, many of which are briefly described herein, I decided that I most wanted to describe the seclusion and beauty found on the CRNRA's many trails. Moreover, many activities such as fishing, rafting, and picnicking require little description for those familiar with the CRNRA. The secrets of the CRNRA are most often revealed when one follows paths deep into the woods.

Another issue presented itself in the form of the sheer number of unmarked trails leading through the CRNRA. The more I walked the trails, the more I became aware of the vast number of unmarked trails, intersections, old wagon and jeep roads, and other paths that crisscross the area. I have tried to limit my trail descriptions to the marked trails that are acknowledged by blazes and/or signs and those that are listed on official National Park Service maps.

When an unmarked trail is described, it will be described as such, or mention will be made of the lack of guiding markings. On some occasions, I will mention intersections with unmarked trails, principally to keep the hiker from taking a wrong turn but also to let the curious reader know where those trails lead. I would encourage the reader to closely observe all Park Service signs relating to trail closure and trail restriction. Closed trails are usually clearly marked with signs, fences, and logs blocking them. Most trails are not open to bicycles, and you will often note signs prohibiting bikes. Open trails are often marked with map signs at junctions. These signs usually contain a copy of the Park Service map of the nearby areas and often are marked to show the sign's reader his or her location. Blue blazes mark many of the open trails covered in this book.

In summary, a reader will find in this book a comprehensive discussion and guide to all the open, maintained trails in the Island Ford Unit and all units south thereof. I have also provided directions to trailheads, brief lists of activities at each unit, a brief list of unique sights at each unit, and a list of facilities available at each unit. Also provided is a summary of the trails described for the reader's convenience.

What to Do

The fun part is deciding what to do at the CRNRA. On any given day, an avid lover of the outdoors will have to choose between hiking, running, mountain biking, road biking, photography, wildlife observation, fishing, paddling, rock climbing, and many other available pursuits inside and just outside the CRNRA. The following is a list of suggestions, many of which are outside the scope of this trail guide. Enjoy!

1. Hiking/Walking

Recently, I have noted an increase in the number of people enjoying a hike or walk along the more secluded CRNRA trails. Almost all the trails are suitable (at least in part) for family rambles with children. I have taken my children on many of these trails, and on occasion, I've pushed a Baby Jogger over CRNRA trails that clearly were not designed for wheeled access. Although some of the trails can be rocky and/or wet, they generally present few difficulties other than rocks and uphill grades. Because many of the trails snake through the deep woods, they remain wet and muddy long after the rain leaves the area. The ubiquitous Georgia red clay can be very slippery after a rain, so come prepared for mud, unless you hike in the dry season. Although CRNRA trails can be wet and muddy, the hiking is often moderate or easy because the CRNRA has few long grades, technical climbs, or stream crossings.

If you decide to hike some of the more remote trails, be aware that there are hazards that warrant attention. Often, the remotest trails are also the most beautiful. But if you have a health condition or have brought small children with you, keep in mind that the access into many of these trails is difficult, even for emergency personnel. I am reminded of this fact whenever I am trail running remote sections of the CRNRA. Rescue from many of the trails in the CRNRA would be difficult and time-consuming. Be careful out there.

2. Trail Running

One of my favorite CRNRA activities is trail running. Many units of the CRNRA are especially suited for trail running for several reasons. First, access is generally easy. Second, the trails are usually well maintained, and uphill grades are short and less strenuous than in the mountains. Third, many loops and side-trail possibilities are present, allowing a runner to tailor a run to his or her needs. The variety of trails and terrain also allows a runner to craft different routes on different days, which avoids the burnout that occurs when one runs the same trail repeatedly. Finally, trail running gives one exposure to a lot of the natural features and beauty of the CRNRA, creating a peaceful yet focused running experience. I have noted in the trail descriptions herein many of the trails that are most suitable for trail running.

If you do decide to run the CRNRA trails, make sure that you run trails that are within your ability, stamina, and training. It's always better to build up to more difficult trails rather than attempt them without building up strength and stamina first.

3. Biking

There are numerous opportunities to bike in and around the CRNRA. Don't overlook them! The Cochran Shoals fitness trail provides a nice ride of a little more than three miles on crushed gravel for riders of all ages and abilities. A tour around the fitness trail can be repeated several times for a better workout and many sightseeing opportunities. The fitness trail can also be combined with a ride up Columns Drive for a longer ride that can also be repeated.

The fitness trail also provides one of the trail access points for a challenging mountain bike ride from Cochran Shoals to Sibley Pond at the Sope Creek Unit. Although this trail includes some mild stretches, it also has some steep climbs and twisting trails that require good mountain biking skills. The Cochran Shoals to Sibley Pond mountain biking trail has undergone some major changes in recent years. A few years ago, the ride was very rocky and difficult, as it followed old roads through the woods. Erosion began to take its toll on the trail. The recent renovations by the Park Service and volunteer organizations transformed the trail into one that is much easier to ride and more erosion-resistant. However, steep grades and tight turns remain. The same renovations also transformed and rerouted many of the other trails in the Cochran Shoals/Sope Creek Unit/s.

Other places to ride include the access road to the headquarters building at the Island Ford Unit and Columns Drive between Johnson's Ferry and the parking lot at the Cochran Shoals Unit. Regardless of your fitness and skill level, you will find biking that meets your needs at the CRNRA. Make sure to wear a helmet while biking, and do not ride a bike on a trail unless it is clearly marked for biking.

4. Boating

Obviously, the river itself presents many opportunities for boating. If you are interested in pursuing boating on the river, you have the choice of raft, canoe, kayak, inner tube, or other means of enjoying the river. I've enjoyed all these types of boats on the river, and each has its unique benefits. There are several access points: the Paces Mill/West Palisades Unit provides a great takeout point for runs on the lower river. A run from the Powers Island put in point to Paces Mill/West Palisades makes for a quick run of an hour or two. This run can be lengthened by putting in at the Johnson's Ferry North Unit. These runs provide some fun shoals and a wave or two in which kayakers can play in high water. One can also extend the run even farther by putting in at Morgan Falls Dam.

The Gold Branch Unit provides access to Bull Sluice Lake, where one can find mild flat-water paddling and exploration. Paddlers on Bull Sluice Lake should be able to spot lots of wildlife, including birds and beavers. The Island Ford Unit also provides access to the river down to the lake and includes some beautiful sections of the river.

If you decide to paddle, please keep in mind that the river can be a dangerous place. Water levels can rise quickly due to rainfall and dam releases. High water levels present extreme dangers to those on the river. A spill into the river also presents many dangers, including cold water, rocks, and holes. Be careful when you're out on the river, and make sure to wear an appropriate floatation device. Also, make sure to read and abide by the regulations and signs.

5. Fishing

Fishing for trout, bass, bream, catfish, and other species can be good in the river through the CRNRA. The Chattahoochee River is the southernmost trout stream in the United States. Its waters are kept cool, usually around fifty-eight degrees Fahrenheit or less, by their discharge from the bottom of Lake Lanier. Some folks choose fly-fishing for rainbow and brown trout using elaborate gear and float tubes. Others just try their luck using everyday spinning gear. Georgia regulations relating to public waters, including licensing, apply to fishing in the river and throughout the CRNRA. Georgia's trout-fishing regulations apply to the river during trout season. Special regulations involving hook use and immediate return to the river of trout apply outside of the regular trout season. Make sure to obtain and read Georgia's fishing regulations before fishing in the CRNRA. Georgia publishes a nice free guide to the regulations that apply to each river in the state that is available in many sporting-goods stores. Please abide by all the rules and regulations relating to fishing in the CRNRA. Make sure that you have the correct fishing license and stamp.

People who fish the river regularly are aware of the holes and structure that hold the most fish. One productive technique is to fish where creeks feed into the river. Also, one can try to look for structure in the river abutting deeper water. Fish hold in these areas. Make sure you know what you are doing before you wade out into the river with your fishing gear. The CRNRA also has several ponds that are frequented by fishermen, although the ponds are often affected by drought conditions in the North Georgia area, which appears to decrease the number of fish in the ponds. For example, there are small ponds at the Sope Creek and Island Ford Units. Make sure to have a valid fishing license for these ponds too. The ponds contain small fish, such as bass and bream. They are ideal locations to teach children how to fish.

6. Wildlife Observation

It is always a special moment when a hiker or runner comes upon wildlife. In my years of exploring the CRNRA, I have been amazed by the wildlife in the area, given that it is surrounded by the metropolitan Atlanta sprawl. Visitors seeking to observe wildlife should come to the CRNRA in the morning or the evening (before the park closes) to have the best chance of seeing animals. Be quiet and be still in order to see more wildlife. Visit areas that are remote or less frequently visited, and spend time around the many bodies of water in the CRNRA. These bodies of water include the river itself, as well as ponds, swampy areas, and beaver ponds. Also, be aware that forested areas make it more difficult to observe wildlife. I have had the most luck seeing wildlife in the spring and in the fall. The Atlanta area can be beastly hot in the summer, and many animals stay deep in the forests to keep cool. In the wintertime, many animals conserve warmth and move around less, but because of the lack of vegetation, some animals such as birds are more easily spotted.

There is an amazing variety of birds that visits the CRNRA. Some of the more interesting species include herons, owls, mallards, Canadian geese, woodpeckers (including the large pileated variety), hawks, cardinals, brown thrashers, indigo buntings, warblers, and many other types of songbirds. I have often seen snowy egrets prowling the wetlands in the CRNRA. I have also seen white swans on the river near the Island Ford Unit, and I've seen owls, such as barred owls, prowling the woods in the Cochran Shoals Unit. The areas around Cochran Shoals, Powers Island, and the Palisades have many blue heron nests that can be observed during the spring and the warmer months. These huge and graceful birds will startle you because of their size if you come upon one silently stalking its prey in the river. Keep your eyes open and alert for the many birds to be seen in the CRNRA, and you won't be disappointed.

Larger animals can be more difficult to locate, but if you spend enough time hiking CRNRA trails, you will see numerous animals. White-tailed deer can be observed in several units, including the Island Ford and Cochran Shoals Units. Twenty years ago, sighting a deer in the CRNRA would have been a very unusual event. However, in recent years, I come upon deer very regularly in some CRNRA units and often see three or more at one time. I have also happened upon a coyote while trail running in the Cochran Shoals Unit. I've seen turtles of many different types, including musk turtles, painted turtles, eastern box turtles, and snapping turtles. Once, I happened upon a turtle nesting in the woods near a stream. On other occasions, I came upon snapping turtles weighing sixty pounds or more crossing the fitness trail at Cochran Shoals. Many snakes inhabit the CRNRA, and I've seen garter snakes, black rat snakes, ring-necked snakes, banded water snakes, and copperheads. Lizards to be seen include anoles, eastern fence swifts, and five-lined and brown skinks.

The wet areas in the CRNRA are home to many amphibians, including toads, bullfrogs, and leopard frogs. An amazing array of salamanders can also be seen by the observant hiker. For instance, I have seen marbled salamanders walking alongside CRNRA trails and, once, found an eight-inch spotted salamander walking slowly across the fitness trail at the Cochran Shoals Unit. The chocolate brown of its skin was highlighted by several bright yellow spots that gave away its location on the trail.

Beavers are regularly seen in the ponds and swampy areas, including Bull Sluice Lake. I have seen many beavers in the wet areas of the Johnson's Ferry North Unit and the Cochran Shoals Unit and often see them in Sope Creek near its confluence with the river. Other smaller mammals, such as raccoon, rabbits, muskrat, foxes, and opossums, are seen mainly at night or in the dusk. On many of my trips, I have observed rabbits in the CRNRA, and they appear to be in abundance in the area during the summer. One good place to spot rabbits is the Johnson's Ferry South Unit. Look in the grass alongside trails and dirt roads.

Also, look in the area streams and in the river for evidence of freshwater mollusks. They can be plentiful. In the summer, one can observe bats feeding in the evenings. Lastly, if you visit the CRNRA, you will definitely see the ubiquitous gray squirrels and chipmunks.

Don't underestimate the opportunities for viewing wildlife in the CRNRA! I am constantly amazed by the variety of wildlife I see there.

7. Rock Climbing

There are some opportunities for rock climbing in the CRNRA. They consist mainly of overhanging cliffs and rock shelters that, in some cases, were used by Native Americans for shelter long ago. Many of the climbs are overhanging and difficult, but the rock is often of fairly good quality. Most of the climbing areas are small, presenting one to five routes. Although I have spent many hours climbing in the CRNRA, instruction in the dangers of rock climbing is far outside the scope of this book. Please be aware that rock climbing is an inherently dangerous and difficult activity that involves specialized safety equipment. You alone are responsible for your safety and the operation and use of your equipment. Please take extreme care in climbing rocks in and around the CRNRA.

8. Picnicking

There are many opportunities for family picnics in the CRNRA. Most of the units have picnic tables that are suitable for family outings. For instance, the West Palisades Unit has picnic tables along the river near the boat takeout, and the Powers Island Unit has picnic tables near the pavilion. The Johnson's Ferry South Unit also has a pavilion with picnic tables. Some units also have benches that can be used for picnics. Other folks just decide to spread out their picnic basket and belongings on a blanket in grassy areas. I would strongly recommend picnics in the spring and fall, when bugs are at a minimum and the sun is still bright enough to warm. However, winter can provide some good, mild days for picnics too, especially in late February and early March. If you take the time to investigate the facilities at each unit, you will find sufficient rustic amenities that will serve your picnicking needs.

9. Family Fun

There are unlimited opportunities for families with children to enjoy the CRNRA. My own children have learned to hike there and have learned much about nature. Most of the trails are well adapted to youthful hikers, and very few of the trails contain inherent dangers for kids, such as drop-offs or potential falling rocks. You can teach your kids to ride a bike on the Cochran Shoals fitness trail. You can play Frisbee in the open areas of the West Palisades Unit. You can push a Baby Jogger over the rocks of the wooded trails as I have done many times (make sure the Jogger has good shock absorbers and big wheels). You can teach your kids to fish in Long Island Creek, Sope Creek, or one of the CRNRA ponds. The possibilities are limitless for those with a family and a vivid imagination.

10. Viewing Wildflowers

If you visit often and keep your eyes open, you will be amazed by the variety and extent of wildflowers in the CRNRA. If you visit the CRNRA in the spring, you will be dazzled by the wildflower variety and color. But many flowers also bloom in summer and in the fall, although they are fewer in number. Some of the more interesting flowers that can be spotted in the CRNRA include flame azalea, rhododendron, mountain laurel, trillium, cardinal flower, iris, goldenrod, bloodroot, passionflower, spiderwort, trumpet creeper, and spotted jewelweed. Low-lying areas are often the best for viewing wildflowers, particularly areas that are wet or near creeks. Toadshade trillium is abundant in many such areas in the spring, and I have observed three species of trillium in the CRNRA (including the uncommon catesby's trillium). If you want to see the largest variety of wildflowers, make regular trips to the CRNRA wetlands from early March to early June. Bring your camera, tripod, and close-up lenses for some outstanding photographs.

Seasons in the CRNRA

One of the best aspects of the CRNRA is that it truly can be visited year-round. The roads and parking areas are always open and accessible (within park hours), and the weather almost never prohibits a visit to hike CRNRA trails. Don't miss a chance to visit on a humid summer afternoon following a thunderstorm or on a crisp winter's morning.

My favorite seasons to hike, walk, and run trails in the CRNRA are fall and spring. However, winter and summer also are nice times to visit. In the winter, Atlanta weather can be quite variable. I've experienced temperatures in Atlanta as low as nine degrees below zero (Fahrenheit) in the winter, but rarely do the temperatures go lower than the twenties. Atlanta's winter weather pattern tends toward two or three days in a row of rain with temperatures in the upper thirties to upper fifties and then two to three days of clear, cold weather with highs in the thirties and forties and lows in the twenties. This pattern gives a winter hiker two opportunities: First, don't miss out on those rainy days. Put on some waterproof clothing and some boots and then walk the trails. The hushed silence of the forest will grow on you. Or put on a warm jacket and take advantage of the clear, cold days. The brilliant sunshine will dispel your winter blahs and make you feel that spring is on the way. Many animals hide during the winter months, but I have seen larger animals such as deer and coyotes during winter runs.

Summers in Atlanta can be sweltering. The heat can be overwhelming, and the humidity is stifling. I've experienced summer temperatures in Atlanta as high as 107 degrees (Fahrenheit). The best time to visit the CRNRA during the summer is in the morning or the evening. You should avoid the CRNRA during summer afternoons, unless it is uncommonly cool or you want to go for a sweaty trail run or bike ride. However, beastly hot days can cool rapidly once the sun goes behind the hills, and evening hikes can be very enjoyable. Bring some bug repellent, and spend time catching lightning bugs or counting the bats swooping overhead. Many animals can be seen on summer evening hikes. Keep your eyes peeled for owls, deer, raccoon, rabbits, herons, and other small animals.

The spring is an exciting time at the CRNRA. Many animals become more active. Leaves begin to cover the trees again. The most springlike months are usually March, April, and May. Spring is a great time to observe wildflowers at the CRNRA, which add beautiful color to a greening forest.

I have spent many days observing and photographing wildflowers in the CRNRA, and I can truthfully say that some of the CRNRA units are incredibly blessed with many colorful wildflowers in the springtime. Some of my favorite units for wildflowers are the Island Ford Unit, the Cochran Shoals Unit, the Johnson Ferry North Unit, the Powers Island Unit, and the Paces Mill/West Palisades Unit. Don't miss the spring wildflower displays!

Fall is probably my favorite time of all in the CRNRA. Although the woods seem sad for the loss of summer and the impending cold of winter, the colorful display of changing leaves in the CRNRA is truly dazzling. Acorns and nuts falling from the many trees also add to the fall scenery. So many Atlantans head for the mountains to see the changing leaves that the roads into North Georgia are clogged with cars for many miles on weekends during October and November. Those same folks are missing some truly great scenery in their own backyards in the CRNRA, which they could have taken in without braving the long lines of traffic! I have spent many afternoons wandering CRNRA trails in awe of the beautiful fall leaf colors along the trails, with colorful acorns hued in yellow, red, green, and brown underfoot. The crisp nip of fall air makes hiking a joy. Plan a day in the CRNRA during late October, and you will not be disappointed.

Rules and More Rules (CRNRA Regulations)

There are many rules and regulations that govern activity in the CRNRA. Like many wilderness lovers, I have a natural aversion to rules and regulations and find them confining. However, the National Park Service generally enacts its rules for a reason, and therefore, we should all follow them. This is certainly not a complete list of all the rules and regulations of the CRNRA, but I will discuss some of the more significant rules for hikers.

First, expect to pay a parking fee if you drive to a CRNRA unit. As of the date of printing, the parking fee at all units is a modest three dollars. You can also buy a yearly pass, which is economical if you plan to come to the CRNRA ten times a year or more. If you do not pay the fee, expect to receive a citation. On many occasions, I have observed National Park Service personnel ticketing cars without parking passes. Also, make sure to park only in legitimate parking spaces. Citations are also awarded to persons who park in areas that are not permitted for parking.

The main rule for hikers is to stay on marked and maintained trails. In doing the research for this book, I realized that the CRNRA is laced with former roads, used trails, and other unofficial paths. In order to reduce erosion and to avoid damaging plant life, make sure to stay on marked trails. In particular, do not shortcut switchbacks when going uphill or downhill. Remember, others will follow your lead. Only ride your bike on trails that are open to bicycling.

Some of the rules are obvious, such as rules against littering. One of the most discouraging things I see in the CRNRA is the amount of litter that folks simply drop on the ground. Fortunately, I have seen many kind souls picking up the trash of others, and on many occasions, I have gone out of my way to clean up litter I have found on the trails. Do not litter—pick up after yourself. Your mother taught you better than to leave your mess for others to clean up. End of story.

Remember that dogs must be on leash, and the leash cannot be longer than six feet. Please clean up after your dog! The Park Service provides handy doggie bags in several locations, but bagging the mess is only half the story. I have seen countless doggie bags sitting beside trails in the CRNRA, waiting for a kind soul to clean them up. Make sure to pack out all litter, including dog litter.

Keep in mind that the CRNRA is a day-use area and is open only from about dawn to dusk. No overnight camping is allowed. Also, make sure to avoid getting trapped in a unit when the Park Service closes and locks the gate at the end of the day.

Finally, please obey all Park Service signs and postings. The Park Service does a good job of letting hikers know whether or not they should be on a trail. Do not hop fences or ignore signs that close trails. Often, the Park Service will close trails by piling sticks and debris on a formerly open trail or by pushing sticks and branches into the ground to form a barrier. Please respect these barriers and signs. They are there for a reason.

Bikers, fishermen, paddlers, and other recreational users have even more rules with which to concern themselves. Hikers have relatively few rules to worry about in the CRNRA. Please obey the rules so that the Park Service does not impose more regulations on hikers.

What to Bring

Hiking stores are replete with gear that a hiker cannot live without. Hiking boots give arch support and traction on mud and rocks. Trekking poles relieve knee pain and provide stability. There are tents, sleeping bags, stoves, packs, sleeping pads, camp chairs, and more for overnight hikers. The list (and cost) can seem endless.

To explore large portions of the CRNRA, very little gear is required. I routinely go for trail runs of up to nine miles in the CRNRA with nothing more than running shorts, running shoes, my car key, my cell phone, and a packet of energy gel. However, some visitors may need other items for fun, safety, or comfort. Selecting gear for a hike can be fun too. Think carefully about what to bring along before starting your journey.

Most CRNRA trails can be easily traversed with tennis shoes or running shoes. However, light hiking shoes can be beneficial in the areas that are rocky or muddy. In the winter and spring, many of the trails that are bone-dry during the summer and fall become quagmires, and boots with good mud traction can be helpful. If you plan on going down into the creek bottoms or playing near the river itself, waterproof boots can be a boon. Some runners and walkers wear the new shoes that mimic barefoot foot support and, thus, develop good foot muscle structure. But most folks at the CRNRA just wear running or walking shoes and enjoy their light weight, comfort, and good support. Obviously, the most important point is that you wear comfortable footwear. If possible, experiment with different shoes to determine what works best for you.

I have seen some folks use trekking poles in the CRNRA. However, the vast majority of hikers leave them at home because the distances traversed in the CRNRA are not usually that great, and there are virtually no difficult stream crossings. Generally, there is no need to use trekking poles on the CRNRA trails, unless you need them to support your knees or to keep you from falling.

Although it is certainly not required, I would recommend that you bring some extra food on any day hike or run. I like to bring a gel packet or jelly beans with me on trail runs. On bike rides, I bring a fruit/nut bar and some gel. On hikes, I may bring several fruit/nut bars in case I get really hungry. Bananas or apples are great snacks that keep well on short hikes. Likewise, you may decide to fill your day pack with a full lunch, including a sandwich, chips, and a thermos. Whichever way you go, just make sure that you have enough calories to keep your stomach from lessening the enjoyment of your hike.

Water is even more important than food. If you are going on a day hike, always carry a water bottle or bladder. Particularly on stifling summer days, water can be a lifesaver. Mixing in some electrolytes can add taste and nutrition to your fluids.

If you are hiking or long-distance trail running, a comfortable backpack will add to the enjoyment of your experience. Make sure it is large enough to hold the gear you intend to carry and that it is comfortable and rugged. Some day packs allow you to keep a water bladder in them and feed a drinking tube out through a hole in the pack. Packs with bladders appeal to those who enjoy staying fully hydrated on a hike or run. Sometimes, a hip or fanny pack is often all that is needed. On the other hand, parents hiking with kids will need all sorts of paraphernalia, including Baby Jogger, diaper bag, burp cloths, toys, baby food, jelly beans, cereal, juice, and other goodies.

One of the items I most recommend that a hiker carry is a waterproof jacket. In the winter, soft rains can last all day in the CRNRA. In the spring and summer, sudden storms can arise with a fury. I find that tucking a lightweight, waterproof jacket into your backpack gives you peace of mind and plenty of protection. Trail runners may be able to skip the jacket. On many occasions, I have gone off on a run several miles into the CRNRA with only shirt, shorts, and shoes, only to be drenched when a massive thunderstorm hits. I find that just running through the storm suits me fine, because the Atlanta temperatures are generally warm enough that hypothermia is not a threat, except in winter. Other folks may not be so receptive to a deluge and should bring along a light jacket for insurance. One other useful tip is to remember to keep your cell phone (and keys) in a ziplock plastic bag to protect them from sudden rainstorms.

Other items a hiker may find useful include binoculars and a camera. Binoculars are particularly useful in the CRNRA because there are so many types of birds that nest and visit the CRNRA, and binoculars can help you spot them and observe their behavior. The CRNRA is a regular nesting area for great blue herons, which are more easily spotted in their large nests high in the treetops with binoculars or similar optical devices. The same is true for many other types of birds at the CRNRA, including songbirds, hawks, and owls. Bring some binoculars and better enjoy the birds of the CRNRA.

A camera can open the door to your photographic talents. Nature photography in the CRNRA can be a fun way to complement a hike. Consider taking your camera whenever you visit the Chattahoochee. Other recommended gears include a map, compass, folding knife, sunglasses, sunscreen, and extra clothing.

Safety

A discussion of safety causes me to pause because this book cannot possibly cover all the mishaps that may occur while hiking, running, or biking the trails in the CRNRA. Everyone who enters the CRNRA is responsible for his or her own safety and should take precautions before going out into the woods. This book cannot possibly keep its readers from all possible harms. However, in order to assist the CRNRA visitor, I will give a brief description of some of the hazards that are routinely found in the CRNRA.

Often, visitors fear wild animals more than any other safety hazard. Although there is an amazing array of animal life in the CRNRA, large animals are generally not to be feared but to be respected. Animals such as deer, coyotes, birds, beavers, and raccoon are generally not dangerous for visitors, unless they are rabid. If an animal is acting strangely or if you have any other reason to suspect that it is rabid, give it a wide berth. Otherwise, you have little to fear from the occasional hawk, opossum, mallard, or squirrel.

Snakes can be a problem, but I have not found them to be a safety hazard. Most snakes that you will encounter will be nonpoisonous. Although nonpoisonous snakes will bite anyone who disturbs them, their bite creates a little more than a flesh injury. Common nonpoisonous snakes in the CRNRA include the black rat snake, garter snake, ring-necked snake, and banded water snake. In my experience, you will see more black rat snakes and banded water snakes in the CRNRA than any other type of snake. Black rat snakes can be very long and have a shiny black sheen to their scales. Often, they have a white or specked white underside. I have often come across them stretched along or across the trail as I run or hike. Wait for them to pass or shove them aside with a long stick. There is little to fear from most black rat snakes, although keep in mind that they can climb trees!

Banded water snakes are often mistaken for copperheads and cottonmouth water moccasins. They are usually found sunning themselves along the rocks near streams and lakes. Although they are not poisonous, they are aggressive and will try to bite when cornered. They are best left alone. Garter and ring-necked snakes pose little problem for adventurers because they are usually shy and nonaggressive. Most other nonpoisonous snakes are not often seen.

I have seen the poisonous pit viper copperhead in the CRNRA, although they do not appear in huge numbers. Learn to identify them, and stay as far away from them as you can. I remember one occasion in which we nearly pushed a Baby Jogger with my son in it over a large copperhead that was sunning on the fitness trail at Cochran Shoals. Only my physical restraint of the Baby Jogger kept it from running over the poisonous snake. Always keep your eyes open for copperheads on CRNRA trails. They have distinctive brown blotch markings that can be easily spotted and a triangular head that holds poison administered through fangs. I have never seen a rattlesnake or cottonmouth water moccasin in the CRNRA. However, I would not be surprised to see either type of snake there, and I have learned to spot and avoid them. Avoid any snake that you cannot identify, and watch where you put your feet and hands! To an alert hiker or runner, snakes are not much of an issue.

Snapping turtles deserve some mention. I have seen numerous large snapping turtles in the waters of the CRNRA, including creeks and beaver ponds. On a couple of occasions, I have seen huge snappers crossing the fitness trail at Cochran Shoals. Give them a wide berth. Snapping turtles can inflict a painful and injurious bite if they are able to reach you. Snapping turtles always bite, so observe them from a distance of six feet or more.

Bees and yellow jackets can also be a problem. I have seen numerous signs posted by the National Park Service warning of yellow jackets in the CRNRA. As you hike or run, watch the ground for bees. Yellow jackets live in small holes in the ground and come out to attack anyone who steps on or near their nest. They deliver painful stings that can hurt and itch for hours afterward. Watch the ground as you are hiking or running. If you see a swarm of bees or a hole in the ground that you suspect may indicate a nest, jump over and then pick up your pace. You may be able to avoid being stung or reduce the number of stings, if indeed you encountered a nest. Everyone who is allergic to beestings should carry proper medication when venturing into the backcountry, including the CRNRA.

There are at least two types of poisonous spiders that may inhabit the CRNRA; however, they are seldom seen. The same is true for other stinging insects such as the saddleback caterpillar. Do not handle spiders, and leave caterpillars alone, unless you are familiar with their type.

I have found that animals and insects pose much less of a hazard in the CRNRA than other safety issues. For instance, statistics shows that falls are one of the most frequent causes of injury in the backcountry. Do not climb cliffs or jump off them into water unless you are absolutely sure of what you are doing. A fall from a cliff can cause terrible injury. Jumping into water can cause a broken or severed spine. The geology of the CRNRA has created many rock shelters and cliffs. Do not get too close to the edge of overhangs, and do not climb any cliff that you cannot climb down.

Falls while walking or running can also be a problem. On many occasions, I have tripped over a root or rock while trail running and rolled or slid down the trail for ten feet or so before coming to a stop. These occasions are a painful reminder that one should concentrate on foot placement while trail running. Falls cannot be completely eliminated, but by reducing the number of falls, you can reduce the chance of serious injury. Make sure that you are aware of basic first aid. If you do fall, do whatever you can to prevent infection. Infections can later become a life-or-death issue.

Lightning and wind can be an issue during summer thunderstorms. Stay away from the river and other water sources during thunderstorms. If necessary, crouch down and assume the proper pose to avoid lightning injury. Stay away from tall trees. Trees can also pose a problem during windstorms. I have seen massive trees fall in the CRNRA during windstorms, and I have often worried about them falling on me. If the wind is a big issue, try to stay out of the deep woods.

Finally, I have become increasingly aware of the possibility of a heart attack or stroke while running or walking in the backcountry of the CRNRA. Often, I run long distances in the CRNRA on remote trails by myself with little in the way of equipment or first aid supplies. Some areas of the CRNRA are remote and do not see much foot or bike traffic. If you will be hiking or running by yourself, at least take a cell phone and be aware of your location so that you can call for assistance if needed. Do not run if you are feeling poorly, and monitor your condition carefully during your excursion. If you start to feel poorly, do not take any chances. Find help or call for aid. Even though the CRNRA is well within the metropolitan

Atlanta area, it can take a long time for emergency personnel to locate you and come to your rescue if you are in trouble deep in the CRNRA woods.

Conservation and Awareness

Conservation is generally a matter of being aware of the effects of your actions on wildlands and on other visitors to those lands. The most important aspect of conservation is to respect the wildlands around you, the plants and animals that inhabit those lands, and other visitors. Rather than memorizing numerous conservation rules, try to be generally sensitive and respectful to others and the wild when hiking in the CRNRA. You will enjoy your visit more, and you will add to the enjoyment of other visitors.

Recitation of a few conservation rules and examples of good practices is helpful to illustrate the type of respectful and concerned attitude that is necessary when hiking. For instance, never cut across switchbacks on a trail. Trails are often built to zigzag uphill via switchbacks in order to cut down on erosion and to make it easier for hikers to traverse the terrain. Cutting across switchbacks causes erosion and doesn't ease one's hiking burden because it is more difficult to cut the switchbacks than to follow them as they wind uphill or downhill.

Pick up all trash, including trash that doesn't belong to you. Don't ride bikes dangerously fast on trails (or above-posted speed levels). Don't disturb wildlife. Don't dig up plants or pick flowers. Keep dogs leashed and pick up their waste. Abide by all rules posted by the National Park Service. All these are examples of rules designed to promote respect for the CRNRA backcountry. Please keep them in mind, and more importantly, keep the spirit of these ideas in your head and heart as you traverse the trails of the CRNRA. Other visitors will be in your debt.

Chattahoochee River shoals.

CHAPTER 2

THE PACES MILL/WEST PALISADES UNIT - CREEK MEETS RIVER

Directions to the Highway 41 Entrance

1. Take I-285 east to Exit 19 (US 41/Cobb Parkway).
2. Travel south on US 41 about 1.5 miles to the CRNRA entrance on the right immediately before crossing the river.
3. From I-285 west, take Exit 20 (US 41/Cobb Parkway); turn left (south) onto US 41, and follow the same directions.

Directions to the Akers Mill Entrance

1. Take I-285 east to Exit 22 (Northside Drive, New Northside Drive, Powers Ferry Road).
2. Turn right onto Northside Drive, and continue to Powers Ferry Road.
3. Turn right onto Powers Ferry Road, and travel 1.5 miles to Akers Drive on the left at the wooden mill wheel.
4. Turn left on Akers Drive, and take the second left turn into the CRNRA entrance road. You will find the parking area on the right just down the road.
5. From I-285 west, take Exit 22, and proceed straight through the first traffic light on the exit ramp to the second traffic light.

6. At the second light, turn left onto Northside Drive, and cross I-285 to the intersection with Powers Ferry Road.
7. Turn right onto Powers Ferry Road, and follow the above directions to the mill wheel.

Activities

- Picnicking
- Fishing
- Family walks
- Boating takeout
- Hiking
- Trail running
- Wildlife observation
- Swimming
- Nearby rock climbing
- Biking on Rottenwood Creek Trail

Trails

- An out-and-back hike of 2.5 miles or more (easy to moderate)
- A pleasant, one-mile forest stroll (easy)
- Three loop-trail possibilities: 1.7 miles (moderate), 2.2 miles (moderate to strenuous), and 3.8 miles (moderate to strenuous)

Unique Sights

- Rottenwood Creek
- Ruins of Akers Mill
- Cliffs along the river
- Rhododendron
- Mountain laurel stands
- Devil's Racecourse Shoals

Facilities

- Bathrooms
- Picnic tables
- Grills
- Raft and boat takeout (Paces Mill)
- Activity field
- Trails
- Multiuse trail
- Seasonal bathrooms along the river

The Paces Mill/West Palisades Unit is a gem that is well worth exploring for nature lovers. The unit consists of about 302 acres of mostly piedmont forest and river floodplain. Most folks use this unit as a takeout point for their rafts, canoes, and kayaks that they put in the river upstream (at the Johnson's Ferry North or Powers Island Units) because the river below Paces Mill is more treacherous and difficult to navigate. Few, however, seem to be aware of the excellent backwoods experience provided for hikers, fishermen, trail runners, families, and wildlife observers. This is a good place to explore if you would like to experience the feel of the North Georgia Mountains without traveling outside I-285. Plus, this unit is far less crowded than the Cochran Shoals Unit just to the north.

There are two access points for this unit: One, the Paces Mill entrance is just off US 41. In addition to the raft/boat ramp, this access point includes picnic tables, grills for cooking, extensive parking, restroom facilities, an activity field, and a concession stand. It is a good access point for families, who can use the picnic facilities and who will enjoy the initial section of the Rottenwood Creek Multiuse Trail. This initial section of the trail is wide, paved, flat, and suitable for toddlers, bikes, and strollers and is the lead-in to the entire remaining trail network. The picnic tables at the Paces Mill trailhead are located under trees near the river and provide families an excellent area to spend time together in an outdoor setting.

The second access point for this unit is along Akers Mill Drive, in the midst of some of Atlanta's most popular apartment homes. Nevertheless, this second access point is less frequently used and gives one the feeling of being out in the woods. It includes no facilities other than parking, trailhead signs, and a trailhead; however, one can follow the hiking trail down to the river where there are seasonal bathrooms. Be aware that this second access point is used by the Cobb County Fire Department to access the river for training during the spring and summer months. It is also used by many high school–age kids in the summer to access the river for swimming and floating.

Although leashed dogs are allowed on the trails in this unit, bicycles are not allowed on the trails, except on the Rottenwood Creek Multiuse Trail. The Rottenwood Creek Multiuse Trail is an excellent short biking experience, although there are some steep hills on the trail. Fishermen seem to enjoy fishing in the lower reaches of Rottenwood Creek, where the creek flows slowly into the river. Wildlife is abundant in this unit. Birdwatchers can enjoy viewing many waterfowl that populate the area around Long Island, which stands amid the river along the Paces Mill access area. On a recent July hike, the author spotted mallard ducks, many varieties of birds, painted turtles, toads, a beaver, and a four-foot-long rat snake that tried to convince its attacker that it was a rattlesnake by coiling up and rattling its tail against the nearby leaves. I was not fooled by this charade and quietly ushered the snake off the trail so that I could pass by.

Trail Option 1
Rottenwood Creek Trail
(2.5 to 3.6 Miles Out and Back—Easy to Moderate)

This recently paved trail provides a unique experience in the Atlanta metropolitan area and the CRNRA, combining easy hiking, a possible biking/running route, historical ruins, and a rushing stream into a nice outdoors package. The trail is about 1.46 miles in length and links up with the 0.4-mile Bob Callan Trail, for a total bike/run/hike of 1.86 miles each way. The fact that the trail is paved allows users the option of biking, hiking, running, or Rollerblading along it. The trail does have a couple of steep hills, though making it more difficult for kids and casual riders. Also, be aware that the connecting Bob Callan Trail passes through a more urban area, having been routed underneath an interstate and a couple of other major roads within its 0.4-mile length.

The multiuse trail also provides a possible access to hike along Rottenwood Creek to the ruins of the old Akers Mill. However, one must leave the multiuse trail and bushwhack along the banks of the creek itself in order to easily access the ruins. Both the multiuse trail and the hike to the ruins are described here.

The paved trail begins to the left of the parking area at the Highway 41 trailhead and proceeds into an activity field. This field and the nearby power cut are two excellent places to spot songbirds. The area also contains wildflowers in spring and stands of blackberry bushes that ripen in the late summer. The trail is flat for the initial section as it skirts the field, crosses the power cut at 0.1 miles, and then enters the forested riverside environment. For about 0.2 miles, the trail follows the river through the floodplain forest. Look for at least one massive pine tree on the right in this flat floodplain section. The paved trail then abruptly travels under the I-75 bridges, where the noise of speeding cars is quite noticeable. After emerging from the bridges, the trail follows the river again for a short distance and then crosses Rottenwood Creek on a steel-and-wood bridge at around 0.4 miles from the trailhead. At or near the Rottenwood Creek bridge, one can access three different trails, which lead to the remainder of the trail system.

Just before you cross the bridge, you will notice an information sign and some nice tables and benches to the left of the trail. This area provides a good place to rest and relax at the intersection of Rottenwood Creek and the Chattahoochee River. It would certainly make an excellent location for a picnic lunch, perhaps transported there via bicycles. Of course, the steady drone of I-75 is still quite present above you at this point, so those wanting a more secluded experience should continue farther into the trail system.

After crossing the bridge over the slow-moving creek, one who desires to follow the Rottenwood Creek Multiuse Trail will turn left immediately after crossing the bridge, rather than follow the bank of the river straight ahead, and follow the paved path along the bank of the creek for about one hundred feet. At this point, the trail splits again near a manhole cover. Continue with the paved path that will be the left fork along the bank of the creek, watching for turtles, beavers, toads, and waterfowl. Along this area of the trail, the creek is slow moving, having been backed up by a concrete spillway at the point where it enters the river. About 0.3 miles from the bridge, the paved multiuse trail will traverse along the creek bank via some wooden boardwalk and then reach the second steel bridge over the creek near a black pipe. The view of the creek in this area is nice, particularly in the fall.

At or near this second bridge, a hiker wishing to proceed to the ruins of the Akers Mill should leave the multiuse trail and begin to hike along the left bank of the creek. Before the multiuse trail was created, a hiker had to cross the stream via the large black pipe and then continue upstream along the banks of the creek. Now, a hiker wishing to proceed upstream to the ruins should pick a point near the second bridge and begin bushwhacking along the left bank of the creek.

Bushwhacking upstream of the second bridge, a hiker will notice that the stream takes on a shoaling and rushing nature that is more akin to the streams of the North Georgia Mountains than a city stream in the piedmont region. The trail is overgrown and difficult to follow at times. However, at no point does it become dangerous, nor are you likely to lose the way. Just follow the creek. On warm days, it may be preferable to walk along the rocks in the creek bed. Watch out for snakes and yellow jacket nests.

The ruins of the old Akers Mill hug a hillside on the left (west) bank (facing upstream) of the creek at a particularly scenic point along the creek. The ruins are about 0.8 miles from the first bridge over the creek and about a half mile upstream from the second bridge. They consist of a fascinating set of rock walls and columns that were the foundations of the old mill. You may need to climb the hillside above the creek and below the multiuse trail to spot the ruins, which are well concealed by the hillside if you are not familiar with these types of ruins.

See if you can spot other evidence of the mill operations along the creek, including the old rockworks of the milldam. The gristmill operated during the latter half of the nineteenth century and produced both flour and corn. During the operation of the mill, many mill workers lived in the area. The ruins of the mill are similar to those in the Sope Creek Unit, which is to be discussed later in this book, but are less extensive. In fact, if you follow all the hikes in this book, you will spot many other remains of homesteads and buildings that mirror the construction of these mill ruins.

After exploring the ruins of the mill, return by taking the same trail along the bank of the creek. The total distance for the hike to the mill ruins and back to the Highway 41 trailhead is about 2.5 miles. Obviously, once one leaves the multiuse trail, the trail to the ruins is not suitable for biking or trail running.

Back at the second bridge over the creek on the multiuse trail, the paved path follows the creek for a short way and then begins a rather steep uphill through a power cut onto the hillside far above the left bank of the creek. The uphill is broken at about 0.88 miles from the trailhead by a sign and benches that provide a runner or hiker with a well-deserved rest area. Have a snack here, and enjoy the view and the trees.

The trail then traverses a couple more uphill grades that bring the trail nearly to the level of the access road at the top of the hill. The view of the access road on the left is blocked, first, by the hillside and then by a retaining wall. The view to the right is much nicer, showing the treed slopes leading down to the creek at the bottom of the ravine. After leveling out very briefly, the trail begins a steep descent back down to the level of the at its scenic point beneath the Akers Mill Road Bridge.

At this point, the Rottenwood Creek Trail ends. There are some nice small waterfalls and rushing shoals in the creek at this point that offset the imposition of the looming Akers Mill Road Bridge. Looking down the valley of the creek, one gets the sense of wilderness in the city. Years ago, the author used to access the creek at this point along Akers Mill Road for swimming, sunbathing, fishing, and general exploring. Of course, the area has changed greatly, and the configuration of the road is completely different than it was in the 1970s.

If you wish, follow the Bob Callan Trail to its end. The Bob Callan Trail is another multiuse trail, so it is also suitable for running, biking, and Rollerblading, as well as hiking. The "Bob" traverses along the side of the creek under the Akers Mill Road Bridge and then bends sharply to the right along with the creek. It then parallels the creek along a boardwalk and goes under I-285. It ends at an old bridge after a slight uphill, where there are benches and signs affording a rest area for weary runners and hikers. The end point borders on a couple of office building complexes near the busy I-75 and I-285 interchange. The parking for the area is in the parking lots for the office buildings.

If you reach this point, you may check out the creek on the other side of the old bridge where the trail ends. There is a trail leading along the creek and the corresponding hillside upstream along the creek. If you are game for more hiking, give it a try to see where it leads. If not, head back the way you came, and enjoy the rushing waters of the creek a second time.

Another interesting feature has been recently constructed in this area. Local governments have recently created an asphalt multiuse trail from the Bob Callan Trail up to and along Akers Mill Road to the Cochran Shoals Unit parking area. The trail runs upward from the "Bob" to the level of Akers Mill Road, parallels the roadside for about a mile (crossing one major intersection along the way), and then bends left under the I-285 interstate bridge over the Chattahoochee River to end in the parking lot of the Cochran Shoals Unit. This multiuse trail squeezes between Akers Mill Road and Interstate 285 for most of its length and has little nature appeal. However, once completed, it will allow walkers, runners, and bikers to travel unfettered between the West Palisades Unit and the Cochran Shoals Unit. This connection will give mountain bikers riding on the Rottenwood Creek Trail access to an extensive, interconnected network of trails at the Cochran Shoals Unit with varied access and terrain and access to rides along Columns Drive. This new trail option is, thus, certainly worth considering when planning a trip to the CRNRA.

Trail Option 2
Pleasant, One-Mile Forest Stroll
(One Mile—Easy)

This is one of my favorite hikes and one I am loath to reveal to readers because I want to keep it all to myself. It is beautiful at any time of the year, but during the fall, it is especially enthralling. In the fall, the colorful trees and leaves provide inspiration to hikers who enjoy the crisp temperatures and blue skies that are characteristic of autumn in Atlanta. Look for giant acorns falling to the ground along this hike. I have spent many a lunch hour walking this trail in the fall, enjoying the last warm temperatures before winter sets in.

Start at the Akers Mill Drive entrance. The trail begins behind the large trail sign at the edge of the parking lot. It slopes immediately downward to a fire road, where you should turn right and duck under the massive Park Service gate. Proceed down the road toward the river. About one hundred yards down the road, there is a split where the road leads to the right and where a trail leads steeply down to the left. Stay on the main road to the right. About a quarter mile into the hike, the road will bend sharply to the left. At this point, look for a marked trail leading to the right down into the woods. If you reach the paved (concrete) portion of the road, you have gone too far and missed the turnoff to the trail.

After making the turn, proceed down a couple of switchbacks to a low area where the trail crosses a small drainage. If you follow the drainage upstream, you will find the remains of an old retention dam, perhaps once holding a retention pond for the nearby residences. Immediately after crossing the drainage, a trail leads off to the right. This trail leads to the top of the hill, where it accesses the trail at its entrance from the apartments and condominiums at the top of the hill. Rather than turning right, continue on the same trail as it winds to the top of the hill through some nice, upland forest.

At the top of the hill, you will reach a T intersection with another trail. To the right, the partially paved trail leads to the apartments and condominiums. Turn left here, and walk slightly uphill along an old gravel road that gradually turns into a trail. This part of the walk is easily the most pleasant and beautiful. It leads along the top of a small ridge through a tall forest dominated by oaks. Take your time, and look around at the trees. Although several major highways are very close by, you can barely hear the road noise, and you can easily envision yourself in the mountains of North Georgia.

Follow the trail until it splits at an old signpost. One branch leads steeply downhill to the left. The other leads gradually uphill and then itself turns steeply downhill. Once you reach the trail split, you can access the rest of the trail system by proceeding, or you can turn around and return to your car. Don't miss the chance to view the fall colors on this hike! It is a great family stroll or lunchtime break from work.

Trail Option 3
Short-Loop Hike
(1.7 Miles—Moderate)

This short-loop hike is a great introduction to the piedmont forest and river floodplain that make up a large portion of this unit. The hike follows the same initial 0.4 miles of the Rottenwood Creek Multiuse Trail to the first Rottenwood Creek bridge. At the bridge, one can turn right (or perhaps more straight ahead) and follow this hike along the river. However, this description will follow the hike in the reverse direction, taking a left-hand turn immediately after the Rottenwood Creek bridge. This hike can be combined with any of the others in this section for loops of varying distance.

After turning left, the hiker will proceed around one hundred feet to the same split in the trail mentioned above. There is a trail sign and map at the split as well as a sewer device. Take the right-hand fork that angles away from the creek. At first, the trail goes through an area that may be muddy after a rain and proceeds slightly uphill through a mature forest near a small rivulet. After about 0.2 miles, the trail begins a steeper climb and becomes rocky. At 0.4 miles from the split with the Rottenwood Creek Multiuse Trail, turn right and downhill at a trail sign on the right. This trail descends steeply for 0.1 miles to the river at a possibly muddy trail junction. There should be another trail sign at this junction. Turn right to complete the small loop. From the junction, the trail parallels the river for about 0.4 miles back to the first bridge over Rottenwood Creek. This section of the trail affords nice views of the river. Look for ducks, herons, and other waterfowl. There are some excellent rocks for sunning and resting about 0.2 miles from bridge. These rocks provide a good view of Long Island Shoals, one of three shoals in the river that are adjacent to the West Palisades Unit.

After reaching the bridge, proceed 0.4 miles back to the trailhead along the multiuse trail. This short-loop trail is quite well suited for trail running and will provide a nice short workout for runners.

Trail Option 4
Medium-Loop Hike
(2.2 Miles—Moderate to Strenuous)

This hike extends the prior loop to include a climb through the cliffs section of trail along the river. Generally, the trail is suitable for trail running, except for the section near the cliffs. This section is a strenuous climb among rocks and bushes that often requires use of the hands to maintain balance and climb up steep slopes. Although the steep section gives this hike its "moderate to strenuous" rating, the difficult section is short, and one can resume trail running once past the steep section.

Although this hike can also be traveled in either direction, it is best followed in the reverse direction as the prior trail description (option 2) so that one climbs up, rather than descends, the cliffs section. The unsure footing in the cliffs area makes descending difficult. To accomplish this hike, follow the previously described 0.4-mile trail from the trailhead to the first Rottenwood Creek bridge on the multiuse trail. At the bridge, proceed straight ahead, and follow the river 0.4 miles along the route of the previous loop hike (option 2), passing the nice rocks along the river about halfway. When you reach the T intersection for the short loop at the trail sign, do not turn left uphill onto the short loop. Instead, proceed straight ahead, paralleling the river.

A short distance from the intersection, you will begin to encounter rhododendron and mountain laurel bushes. These plants are common in the Appalachian Mountains but are very unusual occurring in the wild so far south. The stands of rhododendron plants in this area of the CRNRA may well be one of the southernmost stands of this plant occurring in the wild in Georgia.

At about 0.8 miles from the Rottenwood Creek bridge, you will encounter the cliffs section. Turn to the left, and scramble up the first set of rocks along the river. Be careful not to get too close to the edge. There is a good view of the river from the top of the first set of rocks, especially in winter. After catching your breath, proceed directly uphill away from the river along a steep trail up the ridge through the underbrush. After another short climb, you will come to an intersection of sorts, where a small yellow-and-white sign is affixed to a tree warning "Use caution near the edge." A turn to the right will lead you on the path to the longest loop trail. For this hike, proceed straight uphill along the ridge until the grade becomes less steep. At 0.2 miles from the bottom of the cliffs (although it does seem longer due to the grade), you will reach a trail intersection with another trail sign. Turn left along the rocky wide trail.

The remainder of the hike is a pleasant stroll through upland woods that reminds one of the North Georgia Mountains. The trail is rocky but wide and easy to follow. At 0.1 miles from the junction, you will reach a signpost in the ground where a trail appears to go straight ahead beyond the post. Turn left, and go steeply downhill for 0.1 miles to another trail sign at the junction for the shorter loop. Do not turn left at this junction, but proceed straight ahead for 0.4 miles to the junction with the Rottenwood Creek Trail and the first Rottenwood Creek bridge. At this point, you can return to your car along the 0.4-mile multiuse trail. This loop trail can be combined with the other loops in this section for hikes and trail runs of varying lengths.

Trail Option 5
Long-Loop Trail
(3.8 Miles—Moderate to Strenuous)

This hike is a real treat for nature-starved city folks who are able to navigate the steep cliffs section of the trail. It is possible to run most of this trail; however, the section around the cliffs and another steep section of trail on the return trip probably will require walking or hiking.

This hike shares the introductory 0.4 miles of multiuse trail to the first Rottenwood Creek bridge with the other hikes in this unit. At the far side of the bridge, proceed straight ahead, and follow the river for the additional 0.4 miles of the short loop that parallels the river to the T intersection at the trail sign. At the T intersection, proceed straight along the river to the cliffs section. Climb the initial rocks and then proceed up the ridge away from the river to the intersection of trails at the yellow-and-white sign affixed to a small tree, warning, "Use caution near the edge." At this point, rather than travel farther up the ridge, one should turn right onto an indistinct trail leading through the mountain laurel generally back along and, ultimately, down to the river.

The trail begins to descend back to the level of the river with several sections requiring careful climbdowns. In this area, the trail parallels a small branch, crosses it, skirts through more mountain laurel and rhododendron (which was still blooming in a wet July when the author hiked this trail), and emerges near the river. The trail then passes through some rocky areas and goes under a large overhanging rock cliff shelter. When it emerges 0.3 miles from the intersection at the sign, the trail affords views of a wide bend in the river and the Thornton Shoals. The trail becomes easy to follow at this point, and the hiker should generally follow the trail options that lead closest to the river. There is at least one alternate route in this section that parallels the main route farther from the river.

When you reach the bathrooms (open in warmer seasons), you have the choice of proceeding along the river a short way to a sandy beach area that affords good views of the Devils Racecourse Shoals. The trail generally ends here. Backtracking to the bathrooms, which are about 0.6 miles from the intersection at the cliffs, the hiker should proceed uphill along a forest service road. The hike is steep uphill at several points, and the roadbed/trail is sometimes made of old concrete. The road ultimately leads to the other trailhead in this unit along Akers Drive. However, before reaching the top, one should turn left and downhill at a major intersection at a trail sign. This turn is near the top of the hill where the concrete ends about 0.3 miles from the bathrooms, and one passes three less significant trail intersections before arriving at this point. The remainder of the trail is about 0.9 miles of travel through beautiful, piedmont woods back to the first Rottenwood Creek bridge, which is only 0.4 miles from the trailhead. The trail is rocky and rolls uphill and downhill but is generally not strenuous. You will pass two possible right-hand turns, which you should avoid, and then pass by the two left turns (both with trail signs) for the middle and short loops. The beauty and quiet of this section of trail are more than worth the effort to get there, because it has the feel of a much more backwoods stroll. It is especially nice in the fall, when the leaves are changing, and in the spring. This loop is one of the gems of the metro Atlanta CRNRA.

Sidebar 1
Rottenwood Creek

The author spent many days hiking and exploring along Rottenwood Creek as a teenager, mostly by accessing the creek via the Akers Mill Road Bridge. The author and his friends generally had the creek all to themselves and would spend leisurely days swimming, sunning, fishing, hiking, and paddling around on inflatable rafts. On one of these forays, the author happened upon the ruins of the old Akers Mill and explored those ruins on subsequent visits.

On one memorable occasion, the author and a friend asked to be dropped off at the creek for the usual fun. Because we had no return ride, we had to walk back to our homes, a few miles away. However, we had to decide how to cross the river. At that time, the Powers Ferry Road bridge (inside I-285) had not yet been built, and the only way to safely cross the river was to go under I-285, cross the river on the New Northside Drive bridge (outside I-285), and then cross I-285 again over the bridge at Powers Ferry Landing. The author's choice was to follow this detour;

however, his friend refused to go so far out of the way. Instead, the friend advocated for wading into the river, pointing out that it looked to be shallow all the way across.

As it began to rain, a choice loomed for us. I agreed to attempt the river crossing. A short while later, we found ourselves on a rock, about three-fourths of the way across the river. The water was frigid, and we were hip-deep in the fast current. A deep channel blocked further passage, and we were unable to go back because we couldn't determine the exact passage we took to get to that point. Fortunately, we had our inflatable rafts with us, and we quickly inflated them while standing deep in the frigid water and paddled across the strong current to the other side before hypothermia set in.

Learn from the author's youthful mistake! Don't try to wade across the river. Remember, the water level can rise very quickly! Also, don't forget that the water quality in the river can vary greatly, and river water can quickly infect any cut or wound on one's skin.

Sidebar 2
Rock Climbing

One of the secrets of the Paces Mill/West Palisades area is a nice set of cliffs suitable for rock climbing on the other (southeast) side of the river, which can be accessed easily by a parking area on the northbound side of US 41 at the bridge. A trail leads down to the cliffs, which are up to twenty-five feet high. The area includes an excellent bouldering traverse, a difficult overhanging climb and a moderately difficult face climb. The overhang is rated at about 5.10, and the face climb is rated about 5.6. Both climbs can be accomplished using a toprope setup.

The author spent many hours with friends during the late 1980s at this climbing area, working on technique and keeping in shape for other climbing adventures. Although the author hates to reveal the location of this rock climbing gem, the inclusion of the area in at least two major climbing books renders attempts at secrecy futile. There are several other areas for rock climbing along the Chattahoochee River, some of which are mentioned in this book. Two of these are at the northern (upstream) end of the West Palisades and East Palisades Units. Please keep in mind that rock climbing is a dangerous, difficult, and physically demanding activity that should not be attempted without proper training, equipment, and technique. You are responsible for your own safety at all times at the CRNRA, especially while engaging in dangerous activities such as rock climbing! Also, please respect private property rights of those owning land near the CRNRA.

This wide road/trail leads from the upper Akers Mill entrance into the West Palisades Unit.

Beautiful wide trail leading down into the West Palisades Unit.

Fall foliage colors in the West Palisades Unit.

A typical blue blaze along a trail in the West Palisades Unit.

This old bench is made for resting along the trail in the upper part of the West Palisades Unit.

The trails in the upper West Palisades Unit are often wide and smooth.

More fine walking on smooth West Palisades Unit trails in the fall.

Solitude can be found in the upper West Palisades Unit of the CRNRA.

The trailhead for the Rottenwood Creek Trail is wide and well marked.

Just before crossing Rottenwood Creek, the Rottenwood Creek Trail passes a nice sitting area along the Creek.

This sturdy bridge crosses Rottenwood Creek and leads into the West Palisades trail system.

Slow moving Rottenwood Creek from the bridge right before the Creek enters the river.

The Rottenwood Creek Trail includes several beautiful boardwalks and bridges.

Smooth pavement characterizes many areas of the Rottenwood Creek Trail.

A view of Rottenwood Creek from a bridge on the Rottenwood Creek Trail.

A view of Rottenwood Creek from the Rottenwood Creek Trail.

CHAPTER 3

THE EAST PALISADES UNIT - SHOALS AND MUCH MORE

Directions to the Whitewater Creek Entrance

1. Take I-75 north to the Mount Paran Road exit.
2. At the bottom of the ramp, turn right (east) on Mount Paran Road.
3. Travel about a half mile on Mount Paran Road to Harris Trail.
4. Turn left on Harris Trail, and follow it for about a half mile to Whitewater Creek Road.
5. Turn left on Whitewater Creek Road, and follow it for about a quarter mile to the park entrance on the right.
6. Follow the park entrance road about one-third mile to the small parking area at the river.

Directions to the Indian Road Entrance

1. Take I-285 east to Exit 22 (Northside Drive, New Northside Drive, Powers Ferry Road).
2. Turn right onto Northside Drive, and continue about one mile on Northside Drive to Indian Trail Road on the right.
3. Turn onto Indian Trail Road, and follow it about a half mile to the entrance to the park.

4. Upon entering park property, you will travel about a half mile on a gravel road to the graveled parking area. There are two trailheads: one is at the parking area, and the other is about a quarter mile back up the entrance road on the left as you travel away from the parking area.
5. From I-285 west, take Exit 22, and proceed straight through the first traffic light on the exit ramp to the second traffic light.
6. At the second light, turn left onto Northside Drive, cross I-285, and then follow Northside Drive to Indian Trail Road, as described above.

Activities

- Picnicking
- Fishing
- Family walks
- Boating takeout
- Hiking
- Trail running
- Wildlife observation
- Swimming

Trails

- An easy, out-and-back hike of about one mile to a rock shelter used by primitive peoples (easy)
- A nice, lollipop-loop hike along the river and through uplands of about 1.5 miles (easy to moderate)
- An awesome, out-and-back stroll of about 1.2 miles to an overlook above the river's shoals (easy to moderate)
- A forested walk of about two miles down to the ruins of an old homestead and a bamboo forest along the banks of the river (moderate)

Please note that the trails interconnect, so longer loops and other hikes can be arranged.

Unique Sights

- Large rock shelter used by primitive peoples
- Rhododendron
- Mountain laurel stands
- Long Island Shoals
- Thornton Shoals
- Devil's Racecourse Shoals
- Long Island Creek
- Beautiful overlook high above the river
- Old homestead ruins
- Bamboo forest

Facilities

- Picnic tables
- Grills
- Raft and boat takeout (Whitewater Creek entrance)
- Trails
- Trash cans

The East Palisades Unit is a real opportunity for explorers to find solitude and beauty. Consisting of about 393 acres of piedmont forest and floodplain, there is much here to see and do. The most characteristic feature of this unit is the nearly constant view of shoals and shallow rapids in the river. Moving upstream along the river from the Whitewater Creek trailhead, the hiker will be able to view Long Island Shoals, Thornton Shoals, and then the Devil's Racecourse Shoals. On a warm summer day, the river along the East Palisades Unit will be filled with young people in rafts, tubes, and other watercraft or climbing around on the rocks in the shoals. Their joyous calls can fill the air as they savor the nice contrast between warm sunlight and the cold waters of the river. Vendors along the river during the summer make a rafting adventure an easy playday.

The fall colors can be stupendous in this unit, and the geology is also very interesting. The East Palisades Unit showcases the Brevard Fault, which is a large fault in the earth's crust running, in part, from the northeast corner of Georgia down to Heard County on the border with Alabama. The Chattahoochee River follows the fault through much of its distance. The Brevard Fault is easily seen in the Devil's Racecourse Shoals, which permeate the river with rocks peeking above the surface of the river during its run past the East Palisades Unit. As the river has cut through a high ridgeline of the Brevard Fault, its rocks have been exposed, thus creating the shoals. A viewing platform situated high on a ridge above the river provides a good view of the shoals and the intersection with the fault.

This unit receives a fair number of users but is certainly less frequented than the Cochran Shoals Unit. It has two access point trailheads, which are very different from each other, for visitors. The first access point is along Whitewater Creek Road. It puts the visitor right along the river, where Long Island Creek flows into the Chattahoochee. Walks along the river forest and floodplain begin here. This access point includes a raft/boat launching area, picnic tables, a grill, and trash facilities.

The second access point is at the end of Indian Trail Road. This access point is high on the ridge above the river and allows a hiker to begin a voyage in the piedmont forest where the river is but a distant goal. The Indian Trail access point has no facilities but does include two trailheads for access to the trail system. A trail runs from the Indian Trail access point down to the river near the trailhead at the Whitewater Creek trailhead. This trail is just over a half mile in length. The first third of the trail is a level walk through the forest. The next third of the trail is a moderate drop to the level of the river, which begins near the old foundation of a former homestead. The final third of the trail connecting the two trailheads consists of a level walk along Long Island Creek. Each of the two access points has its benefits, but the contrast between the two is notable.

Bicycles are not allowed on the trails in this unit. Fishing is possible among the various shoals running through the river in this unit, and fish sometimes congregate in the area where Long Island Creek flows into the river. Many animals and birds can be spotted in this unit, and the wildlife here is similar to that found in the West Palisades Unit on the other side of the river. Deer are now frequenting this unit, and other animals such as foxes, lizards, and beavers can also be seen. Along the river in the upstream sections of this unit, one can find numerous trees that have been gnawed by beavers. Keep your eyes open for animal encounters.

Trail Option 1
Rock-Shelter Hike
(1.0 Miles Out and Back—Easy)

This short hike provides the chance to see a large rock outcrop that was probably used by primitive peoples for shelter. The hike is easy, except for the final short climb up to the rock shelter. This is a hike that anyone interested in archaeology would find fascinating.

The hike begins at the Whitewater Creek trailhead. After exploring the trailhead, take a short stroll down to the river at the raft and boat ramp to gain a view of the river and the Long Island Shoals. Then return to the trail signs, and follow the trail behind them onto the nice metal bridge over Long Island Creek. As you cross Long Island Creek, look down to spot small bass and bream that make the creek home. At the far side of the bridge, you will reach a signed trail intersection. Take the left fork, and follow it over another small wooden bridge.

As you hike, notice the size of the trees in this area along the river. Some of them are quite large. At 0.1 miles, you will reach a view of the river, and you will have intermittent views of the river and its shoals for the next half mile. Although the noise of car traffic from I-75 and Highway 41 can initially be heard, it will fade as the hike progresses.

At 0.2 miles, you will cross another small wooden bridge near a large magnolia tree. At 0.38 miles, you will reach a bench, where you can take a break in the shade of the riverside trees. There is a nice view of the river and its shoals from the bench and the nearby riverbank. Shortly after the bench, you will reach a metal bridge over Charlie's Trapping Creek at 0.46 miles. When I hiked this trail recently in the summer, Charlie's Trapping Creek was dry, but I imagine that during the winter and spring, water flows well here.

Just after crossing the metal bridge over the creek, you will arrive at a signed trail intersection. Take the right-hand trail away from the river. Walk about twenty yards up this trail until you come to another signed trail intersection. At this second intersection, take the left-hand trail along the base of the hill. In about fifteen yards, you will reach a wooden bridge or boardwalk. After crossing this small wooden bridge, look up to the right. You will see the large rock shelter on the cliff above the trail. It can be reached by scrambling up the steep user trail leading to its entrance. If you like, scramble up the hillside like a mountain goat to get a closer look.

According to an article in *Brown's Guide to the Georgia Outdoors*, which is no longer in print, this rock shelter is about seven thousand years old. Apparently, researchers from the Southeastern Archeological Center in Tallahassee, Florida, determined that this rock shelter was made by native people of the early archaic period some seventy centuries ago. It was gradually enlarged to its present size when those natives built fires that expanded the stratified rock. The rocks broke off in layers with the heat of the fires. According to the same article, it is virtually impossible to determine whether the shelter was used as a permanent dwelling by the native people or as a campsite for wandering hunters.

Observe this site with respect for its age and history. Do not vandalize it or remove any rocks or artifacts. Vandals have destroyed many of the archaeological cues that scientists need to investigate the history of this site. Your respectful behavior will be appreciated by other visitors in the future, who will come here for solitude and a glimpse of history.

When you have finished looking over the rock shelter, return to the Whitewater Creek trailhead as you came. If you have more time, explore the various trail options nearby. The trails interconnect and provide many avenues for the explorer.

Trail Option 2
Nice Lollipop-Loop Hike along the River and through the Forest Suitable for Kids
(1.5 Miles—Easy to Moderate)

I took all three of my kids (ages five to ten) on this hike, and they had loads of fun. It is just long enough for the kids to have a good little workout in the woods, but not so long that they will begin complaining about it being too arduous. The kids particularly enjoyed watching the fish in Long Island Creek and chasing lizards sunning themselves in the undergrowth on a warm summer day. Look primarily for anoles, skinks (brown and five-lined), and eastern fence swifts.

This hike begins with the same route as the previous hike. Cross the metal bridge over Long Island Creek, and walk along the pleasant riverbank until you cross the small metal bridge over Charlie's Trapping Creek. After crossing the bridge, you will come to a signed intersection. Bear left at the intersection continuing along the riverside. At 0.58 miles, you will see sluice rapids in the river to your left, and shortly thereafter, you will proceed along a side channel in the river. Side channels such as this one are quiet areas of the river that often contain fish, birds, and animals who come for shelter, food, or water. On one recent trip, my kids and I came upon a fly fisherman in this side channel trying for trout.

At 0.64 miles, you will reach yet another signed trail intersection where a trail comes in from the right. If you turn right, the trail will take you back to the old rock shelter discussed in the previous section. Instead, bear to the left at this intersection. You will very shortly come to another trail intersection; this one, unmarked. The unmarked trail leading to the left follows the riverbank, whereas this hike proceeds directly ahead up a steep, uphill dirt slope. At 0.71 miles, you will reach another marked intersection, at which you should proceed uphill and to the right. The trail will double back up the hill and will also run along the hillside for a way, providing a good view of the forest.

At 0.81 miles, you will reach yet another signed intersection. Again, proceed uphill and to the right at this intersection. You will now be contouring along the hillside above the river. You will go through a nice stand of mountain laurel at around 0.84 miles, following which you will reach a signed intersection at 0.87 miles. Proceed straight through this intersection, avoiding the marked trail to the left and the used trail to the right. Enjoy the nice forest in this section of trail. It provides a nice example of eastern forest, which is perfect for a stroll in the fall or spring.

At 0.93 miles, the trail will begin to roll downhill back to river level. You will reach a step down over a broken tree at about one mile, and at about 1.07 miles, you will reach the bottom of the hill and a marked intersection at which you will proceed to the left. Shortly thereafter and at about 1.11 miles, you will reach a final marked intersection at which you should turn left and cross the metal bridge. Proceed back along the riverside trail to the end of the trail at the Whitewater Creek trailhead, where your car awaits you at the other end of the metal bridge over Long Island Creek.

If you have kids or a dog, this hike is one that they will enjoy without becoming overwhelmed because the distance is manageable and the scenery fairly nice. It can easily be combined with trail option 1, because in two spots, the loop comes very close to the old rock shelter described in the preceding section.

Trail Option 3
Awesome Out-and-Back Stroll to Overlook of River
(1.2 Miles—Easy to Moderate)

This is a hike unlike any other in this unit. It traverses the forests and mountain laurel stands on the ridges above the river until it reaches a nice overlook platform giving a serene view of the river shoals below. This is another fine walk that is suitable for kids and can make a great family outing on a spring or fall afternoon.

The hike begins at the Indian Trail Road trailhead. From the gravel parking area, do not proceed down the trail behind the trailhead signs. Instead, walk 0.21 miles back up the gravel entrance road to reach another trailhead on your left. Turn down this trail through a mature forest. This is a beautiful place to be in the fall.

The trail starts out as an old dirt road blocked by a large rock and is initially easy to follow. At 0.31 miles, the trail stops descending near a used trail that cuts off to the right and enters more rolling terrain. Many tree roots punctuate the trail in this area, so watch your step. Beginning at 0.45 miles, you will reach three marked intersections in quick succession. At the first marked intersection, go left, following the blue-blazed trail. At 0.49 miles, go right at the second marked intersection, and at the third marked intersection at 0.51 miles, go straight. You will eventually proceed steeply downhill along some stairs to the overlook platform above the river.

This platform is an excellent place to take a break. When I brought my kids here, they enjoyed climbing all over the rocks below the platform. I busied myself with enjoying the view and dispensing snacks and water to the troops. From the platform, the river is easily seen below. Although the view is partially blocked during the summertime by foliage, during the winter, the full view opens up. You can also see several tall buildings from this platform. I couldn't help but wonder how many folks were working in cubicles or in offices in those buildings while my kids and I were enjoying the trail. Also evident in the river below are the shoals caused by the geologic phenomenon called the Brevard Fault.

According to a plaque on the platform, it was constructed by Eagle Scouts as a service project. Thanks to them, the platform is well constructed with benches for relaxation. As you recline on the benches, notice the surrounding hillside, which is filled with mountain laurel stands. These bushes are more characteristic of the North Georgia Mountains. Come here in April and May to see whether they will produce their characteristic beautiful white blossoms.

After you have had your fill of the view and the surrounding area, leave the platform by going directly to the left, following the blue blazes as you skirt the hillside through the mountain laurel. At 0.64 miles from the parking lot, you will reach a signed intersection at which you should proceed to the left and downhill. At 0.67 miles, you will reach another signed intersection where you should proceed to the right and uphill. Note the beautiful wooded cove to your left as you traverse this section of your walk.

At 0.74 miles, you will reach another signed intersection where you should turn left and downhill, retracing your earlier steps toward the park's entrance road. Enjoy the forest walk until you reach the gravel road at 0.97 miles, and then enjoy the stroll back to the parking area at 1.2 miles. Take this walk whenever city life is closing around you and whenever you need solitude and perspective. Or go for fall colors and acorns or spring flowers. This is a hike that is unique for this part of Atlanta.

Trail Option 4
Forest Route to Old Homestead and Bamboo Forest
(Two Miles—Moderate)

This is an enchanting walk through beautiful forests that can be considered one of the best in the CRNRA. It leads down to the river, where one can explore the ruins of an old homestead on the banks of the river and stroll upstream to gawk at a bamboo forest containing huge bamboo trees. The hike can be divided into four sections. The first section follows the gravel entrance road. The second section goes through the upland forest, showing off numerous large trees. The third section is a sharp drop down to a creek channel that flows into the Chattahoochee. The final section of the trail follows the creek channel down to where the creek enters the river. The hike is an out-and-back hike of just over two miles.

It begins at the Indian Trail Road trailhead, where there are parking facilities, trash cans, and a major trailhead. However, this hike, like trail option 3, starts out by following the gravel road back toward the entrance to the CRNRA. As you follow the gravel road and watch for cars, glance to either side to view the size and selection of trees on this ridge high above the river. At about 0.2 miles, you will reach the signed trailhead on your left, which will be obvious and blocked by a large rock. Proceed down the trail through the forest, which is truly beautiful in the fall.

There are numerous user trails along this hike, usually leading off to the right as you proceed toward the river. These user trails should be avoided as the existing route marked by the National Park Service is a fine trail, and there is no advantage to following the user trails unless you simply want to explore. Often, these user trails are more difficult because they lack switchbacks, and they certainly contribute to erosion. The National Park Service route is easily followed and blue-blazed for nearly the entire route, although sometimes, the blazes are sporadic.

After entering the forest, you will follow the trail as described in trail option 3. The trail will dip gently to a saddle and then rise slightly uphill. Along the rise, you will reach the first signed trail intersection at about 0.45 miles from the parking lot. Proceed to the right, down a trail that skirts a beautiful cove to the right. After a short distance and about 0.55 miles from the parking lot, you will reach another signed trail intersection. Proceeding straight ahead will lead you to the platform high above the river described in hike 3. However, you should turn right and go downhill toward the river at this intersection rather than straight ahead. The descent will be steep in places and occasionally rocky, but the well-worn trail is easy to follow. There are some switchbacks, and there are also a few mountain laurel bushes along the lower reaches that are probably attractive in the spring. Those who are unable to hike a steep, uphill or downhill trail will not like this section, but it is mercifully short at about a quarter of a mile.

At just over three-fourths of a mile from the parking lot, the trail bottoms out at a nice little creek, where there is a wooden bridge to traverse the trickling stream. In a few short steps, a user trail leads off to the right and back uphill along the creek. Avoid the user trail, and stay on the proper path. The trail crosses an intermittent (often dry) stream via a ford and then climbs up onto the hillside on the northern side of the creek. At 0.87 miles, you will reach another signed intersection. Proceed straight and downhill rather than to the right and uphill.

The remaining trail tracks along the little creek as it winds its way down to the river. Part of this trail is on an old roadbed, and there is another wooden bridge traversing the creek just before you reach the river. If you are hiking with kids, make sure that they check each bridge for trolls before proceeding across to the other side. At just over a mile, you will reach the river where the little creek flows into the Chattahoochee. There is much to be seen here, so plan to spend a little while along the banks of the river. Perhaps a picnic would be fun.

At the junction where the trail reaches the river, you will find the foundations of an old homestead to your left. Take time to explore the ruins, including the stairs leading up to the foundation. According to *Brown's Guide to the Georgia Outdoors*, a civil war battery was located near here. However, the existing house foundations appear to date from the early 1900s. You will also find a cute stone bridge in the trail upstream, where it crosses the little creek. The river is also scenic at this point, so take the opportunity to go to the riverbank for the view. The trail downstream goes for less than a quarter mile before it becomes difficult to continue due to cliffs. Upstream, the trail passes over a wood bridge over a second creek and then enters a large bamboo forest. The bamboo in this area is larger than any the author has ever seen in the Atlanta area. Many of the bamboo shoots are as large as trees, and looking up at their tops gives one the feeling of vertigo. Don't miss this fascinating forest along the river!

Take your time, and wander through the bamboo forest quietly, and then return along the trail the way you came. Remember that the hike will be significantly more strenuous on the way back due to the ascent back to the trailhead from the riverbank. Enjoy.

Sidebar 1
Long Island Creek

Long Island Creek is near and dear to my heart. The creek passes by not far from my childhood home several miles upstream where it spills casually into the Chattahoochee River. When, as a boy, I discovered the creek, my days began to be filled with exploring it. I found another world in that creek, a world that, no doubt, exists no longer. I saw bass, bream, and shiners that would eagerly take my hook. I saw massive snapping turtles moving about below the water, looking for fish. I found large crayfish scuttling about for their next meal.

Most unusual was the annual spring run of white suckerfish that spawned in the rapids of the creek. My friends and I would be casually walking down the stream and disturb a nest of suckerfish, some of which were twenty inches long or more. The fish would thrash about in the rapids, searching for any spot to hide from us. The first time that happened, it scared us witless. After that, we learned to look for the telltale signs of the sucker spawn in the rapids during the spring. One could scout the rapids from a way off, watching for the splashing and fins above the surface of the water that signified spawning suckers.

My buddies and I would spend summer day after summer day fishing the creek. Often, we would walk miles barefoot in the stream. The stream took good care of us—we never cut our feet despite years of opportunities to do so. Sometimes, we would catch literally hundreds of fish from the creek, most of which were tiny. But the thrill of the catch was always there. Armed with nothing more than a pole, a tackle box, and a ball of bread, we felt ready for anything the creek could send our way.

Maybe someday, I will take my kids down to the stream to fish. I doubt that the fishing is as good now as it was. But even a few fish are enough to put a light in the eyes of a child.

Sidebar 2
East Palisades from the North

I have a confession to make. Spurred on by past guidebooks in my collection of literature, I spent an afternoon attempting to access the East Palisades Unit from the upstream end at Ray's on the River. I don't recommend that others make a similar attempt.

In the first place, the area is clearly not set up to be a trailhead. Recent changes to the businesses and dwelling units in the area have made parking difficult or impossible. I'm sure that Ray's needs its parking spaces for its own clientele. Second, there are clear indications that others have tried to restrict access via this route in the past. For instance, there is a fence blocking the way that has been torn down by vandals in one spot to allow trail users to pass through it. Third, there are no indications that the National Park Service has any intention of encouraging folks to access the unit from this direction.

Finally, there is the difficulty of traversing the trail from the north. In two places, the trail ends at rock cliffs that must be traversed in order to proceed. On both occasions, I was able to climb up the cliffs by finding weaknesses in the bluffs and then descend back to the riverbank on the far side of the cliffs. However, I would not recommend this to any but the hardiest adventurer. Watch your step whenever you climb cliff bands at the Chattahoochee, and remember that you must be able to climb back down the same way you climbed up, unless you have another escape route in mind.

The route is no longer blazed and should not be considered to be a functional trail, although I did find some light blue dots on a few trees and other evidence that a trail once existed here. In the end, my traverse spit me out into the bamboo forest described above, where I crossed the wooden bridge and then the cute stone bridge to reach the old homestead by the river. However, this area is more easily reached by parking at the Indian Trail Road trailhead. Be wise, and follow the established route!

The biggest rock shelter found in this book is in these cliffs in the East Palisades Unit.

A closer look at the huge rock shelter in the East Palisades Unit.

Young hikers explore the cavernous rock shelter in the East Palisades Unit.

This sturdy bridge spanning Long Island Creek is one of the entrances to the East Palisades Unit trail system.

Young hikers explore the beach where Long Island Creek meets the Chattahoochee.

Views of the river such as this one open up along the riverside trail in the East Palisades Unit.

This spectacular vista can easily be yours in the East Palisades Unit.

This bridge leads towards the East Palisades Unit from the north.

The river crosses many shoals between the East Palisades Unit and the West Palisades Unit.

Young hikers enjoy downed trees along a trail in the East Palisades Unit

The views of the river abound in the East Palisades Unit.

The trail approaches the bamboo forest in the East Palisades Unit.

This wooden bridge crosses a tributary near the remains of an old settlement along the river in the East Palisades Unit.

CHAPTER 4

THE POWERS ISLAND UNIT - SMALL BUT BEAUTIFUL

Directions

1. Take I-285 east to Exit 22 (Northside Drive, New Northside Drive, Powers Ferry Road).
2. At the top of the ramp, go straight through the traffic light.
3. At the next traffic light, turn left onto New Northside Drive, and cross I-285.
4. Go through two traffic lights onto Interstate North Parkway. The Powers Island Unit parking area will be 0.6 miles on the right, immediately before crossing the river.
5. From I-285 west, take Exit 22 (Northside Drive, New Northside Drive, Powers Ferry Road).
6. Go right at the top of the ramp at the light.
7. Go straight through the next light onto Interstate North Parkway. The Powers Island Unit will be 0.6 miles on the right, immediately before crossing the river.

Activities

- Picnicking
- Fishing
- Family walks

- Boating put-in and takeout
- Hiking
- Trail running
- Wildlife observation

Trails

- An out-and-back hike on Powers Island itself of less than one mile (easy)
- A loop/out-and-back trail of about 1.5 miles (moderate)

Unique Sights

- Ruins of walls and buildings

Facilities

- Pavilion
- Picnic tables
- Raft and boat takeout (on Powers Island) trails

The Powers Island Unit is a small unit, but it is less frequently used for hiking than some other units and, thus, warrants exploration by those seeking solitude. It has a cozy feel about it and, for that reason, is one of my favorite units. It is across the river from the more popular Cochran Shoals Unit, and its parking lot is used for overflow parking whenever the Cochran Shoals parking lot is filled with cars. Instead of following the crowds, why not spend a day exploring the Powers Island Unit? There is a nice short ramble onto Powers Island itself, and there is another series of trails that go along the riverbank and into a beautiful hardwood forest. This latter set of trails is one of those areas that will remind you of the mountains. It also holds some interesting bits of history. Don't miss it.

Trail Option 1
Short Out-and-Back on Powers Island
(0.8 Miles—Easy)

The first area to explore in the Powers Island Unit is the island itself. This is a very short hike, but be prepared to see a lot of wildlife, especially waterfowl. The trail begins near the pavilion area with one hundred feet of paved asphalt trail to a metal bridge spanning a portion of the river. While crossing the bridge, you may notice kayak/canoe slalom gates to the right and to the left. These were in disrepair when I traversed the bridge, but they indicate that this area has been used for training paddlers in the past. At the far end of the bridge (on the island), you will see a kayak/canoe launch area on the right. This is a good put-in to paddle down to the West Palisades takeout in a kayak. Rafts should launch from the other side of the island.

After crossing the bridge, the trail becomes dirt and leads about two hundred feet diagonally across the island to a concrete access point on the river for rafts and other watercraft. There are some nice benches located here from which you can observe the river. Interstate 285 and its access roads are also easily seen (and heard) from this part of the island. From this last river access point, a quiet trail leads to the right (upstream) to the upstream tip of the island. This is not an official trail, and it is not maintained by the National Park Service. But it is an excellent trail for viewing wildlife. You should reach the tip of the island in about a third of a mile. On a recent November trip to this trail, the author came upon many birds at the tip of the island, including a great blue heron, a redheaded woodpecker, Canadian geese, male and female mallard ducks, blackbirds, and other species of ducks.

This journey is worth taking for the possibility of seeing wildlife alone. Plus, this trail is short enough to be combined with many other excursions in the area and is infrequently visited. The end of the island also gives one a unique perspective in viewing the river.

Trail Option 2
Loop/Out-and-Back Trail
(1.5 Miles Total—Moderate)

This is the main hiking route in the Powers Island Unit. It provides a nice variety of hiking and walking for a casual stroll or a more complete exploration of the area. Should you be more interested in a casual stroll, stick to the lowland areas around the river floodplain, and avoid the loop that goes back up the hillside into the forest. However, the forest loop is not to be missed for those who are more intrepid.

The trail along the river floodplain is basically a wishbone shape, with the start of the hike at the lower right (easternmost) prong of the wishbone. This prong starts out into the forest away from the river rather than along the riverbank. The loop trail into the forest on the hillside above the river, which is discussed in detail below, leaves on the right (or eastern) side of this prong of the wishbone-shaped floodplain trail just before the two prongs converge. The entire trail system should not be missed for many reasons, not the least of which is the extensive evidence of past history that can be observed along this trail.

It all begins at the main trailhead at the northeastern corner of the parking lot beside a sign and historical marker in front of the National Park Service gate. The other trail access is near the river at the northwestern corner of the parking lot, and if you follow this hike to its completion, you will end your hike there. For now, proceed from the main trailhead past the gate onto a wide gravel trail that is occasionally wet, which appears to be a remnant of an old road. Although the trail is wide and easy, visitors cannot ride bikes on any of the trails in the Powers Island Unit. Solely foot travel is allowed.

If you read the trail sign before you begin your hike, you will discover that James Power settled on this eastern side of the Chattahoochee River in 1831. Power was a blacksmith and a gunsmith by trade, and he repaired guns for settlers and the Cherokees. He operated a ferry in this area. In 1833, when the Cherokee lands were taken, Power moved across the river to the Vinings area and built a plantation there. However, he kept up the ferry until it was replaced by a bridge in 1903. Keep this history in mind as you hike this trail, and you will find many hints of past settlers in this area.

The first part of the wide trail rolls through a nice forest and in and out of some creek drainages that can be wet at times. In the spring, many wildflowers bloom here, and some wildflowers can also be seen in the fall. At 0.18 miles into the hike, you will cross a very small creek, and shortly thereafter, you will pass some large rock outcrops on the right. Here, you will find some English ivy, which is more prevalent along the trails in this unit than in other units. Perhaps the ivy is but another bit of evidence that humans lived and worked here in the not-so-distant past.

At about 0.26 miles into the hike, you will reach the first of three signed trails heading off up the hillside to the right. These lead to the loop trail discussed below. If you are merely out for a nonstrenuous short stroll, bypass these trails, and proceed straight along the wide floodplain path, crossing another tiny creek drainage. At 0.31 miles, you will reach a signed trail going to the left. This is the second prong of the trail on which you will be returning. Do not take the left-hand turn, but proceed straight ahead. Just past this intersection, a side channel of the river comes into sight. This is a good area to spot Canadian geese. The author has also spotted many songbirds such as warblers in the woods here in the past.

At 0.37 miles, you will pass by some large rock outcrops on the right, and shortly thereafter, you can begin to discern the beginnings of a rock wall running along the right side of the trail. The ruins of the former Puckett homesite are located near here. Be sure to inspect the construction of this rock wall, which is typical of the construction of homesites in this area from the early 1900s. If you follow the rock wall along the trail, at one point, you will see a faint old trail or road leading steeply up the hillside to the right. If you follow it a short distance up the hill, you will find the stone foundations and bits of debris that are the only remains of this former homesite. Please be respectful of the private property signs in this area and do not trespass. When the author last hiked here, posted signs made it clear where the trail ends near the old homesite about 0.44 miles from the trailhead. Turn around and head back the way you came. Be sure to check out the riverside stands of bamboo in this area before leaving.

You will again reach the trail split at around 0.58 miles. Proceed to the right here, closer to the river. Shortly after taking the split, look to the left through the trees. You should be able to spot an old chimney in the woods, where there is a foundation from yet another old homesite. Take time to explore it, if you can find it. Many people miss this old homesite, which is not evident from the trail, except in winter. The trail then follows along the riverside through blooming spring wildflowers and moist, sandy soils. Take time to inspect the riverside for birds, including quiet great blue herons and noisy Canadian geese. You will traverse five small bridges on the way to the parking lot, all crossing small creek drainages from the upper woods. The first three bridges are wooden affairs; the fourth, a steel bridge, and the final bridge is wooden. Upon arrival at the parking lot, turn left to return to the trailhead and your car.

If you have decided to explore the upper woods via the loop trail, take one of the first right-hand turns off the main trail at about 0.26 miles into the initial hike. You will wander through a beautiful cove forest area, which can be wet in the springtime. After crossing a small bridge over a rivulet, you will pass near some rhododendrons and then begin climbing the hillside. You will climb for the next 0.25 miles to the top of the cove and emerge near some buildings that are hidden by the trees in the summer. On your way up the hillside, you will, at one point, cross over the remains of another rock wall, obviously built by past settlers in this area. Once again, take time to examine the wall, which closely resembles the one near the Puckett homesite.

If you are feeling very intrepid, you can find the remains of an old well or pump house nearby. After reaching the top of the arm of the ridge on which the old wall rests, drop down into the drainage that runs on the other (far) side of the same arm of the ridge. While hiking here, I was attracted to this area by the loud croaking of frogs coming from this boggy area. This area can be very wet and requires a short bushwhack down through the undergrowth. But it is worth visiting yet another remainder of the history of this area. A similar structure can be found in the Island Ford Unit. You will note the abundance of English ivy in the vicinity of the old wall too. Also, there is a faint trail to the right in this area, but you should proceed straight instead on the more clearly defined trail up into the cove.

As you ascend, you will see some very large trees to the right. When you reach the top of the ridge, you will head uphill for a short way and then begin a downward long drop back down to the river floodplain. Some of the downward drop is quite steep, so watch your step. When I hiked here, a huge oak had uprooted and fallen across the trail, blocking easy passage. This is further evidence of the damage that wind can cause to the forest. Many of the thunderstorms in the spring and summer produce violent winds and downdrafts that uproot the mature trees in the forests along the Chattahoochee River that are less firmly rooted. Generally, these fallen trees are only noticed later, once they have blocked trails or other CRNRA facilities. Trail maintenance crews remove them or cut paths through them. But more fall every year.

As you near the floodplain, you will reach the moister areas near the bottom of the creek drainage that you have been circling. Look for wildflowers in the spring in this lower bottomland area. At about 0.67 miles from the beginning of the loop trail, you will reach the wishbone-shaped floodplain trail at a point slightly farther north than where you entered the loop. Proceed back to the parking lot via either prong of the trail in the floodplain. The loop trail is definitely a wonderful opportunity to get away from it all without exerting much effort or traveling far from I-285. I would recommend it for anyone who is pressed for time but who wants to feel the spirit of the forest.

Flowers such as these in the Powers Island Unit abound in the CRNRA.

The main trail in the Powers Island Unit starts off as a wide path through the forest.

A portion of the historical rock wall ruins in the Powers Island Unit.

CHAPTER 5

THE COCHRAN SHOALS/SOPE CREEK UNIT - CROWDS AND SOLITUDE

Directions to the Cochran Shoals Entrance

1. Take I-285 east to Exit 22 (Northside Drive, New Northside Drive, Powers Ferry Road).
2. At the top of the ramp, go straight through the traffic light.
3. At the next traffic light, turn left onto New Northside Drive, and cross I-285.
4. Go through two traffic lights onto Interstate North Parkway. The Cochran Shoals Unit parking area will be 0.7 miles on the right, immediately after crossing the river. The parking area just before the river is for the Powers Island Unit.
5. From I-285 west, take Exit 22 (Northside Drive, New Northside Drive, Powers Ferry Road).
6. Go right at the top of the ramp at the light.
7. Go straight through the next light onto Interstate North Parkway. The Cochran Shoals Unit will be 0.7 miles on the right, immediately after crossing the river. The parking area just before the river is for the Powers Island Unit.

Directions to the Columns Drive Entrance

1. Take I-285 east to Exit 24 (Riverside Drive).
2. Turn left onto Riverside Drive, and cross the bridge over I-285.
3. Travel about 2.2 miles north on Riverside Drive until, after a steep downhill curve, you reach the stoplight at Johnson's Ferry Road.
4. Turn left onto Johnson's Ferry Road, and travel 0.25 miles, crossing the river. Immediately after the river is a stoplight at Columns Drive.
5. Turn left onto Columns Drive, and proceed 2.5 miles to the trailhead at the end of Columns Drive.
6. From I-285 west, take Exit 24, and turn right onto Riverside Drive.
7. Follow the same directions above.

Directions to the Sope Creek Unit Entrance

1. Take I-285 east to Exit 24 (Riverside Drive).
2. Turn left onto Riverside Drive, and cross the bridge over I-285.
3. Travel about 2.2 miles north on Riverside Drive until, after a steep downhill curve, you reach the stoplight at Johnson's Ferry Road.
4. Turn left onto Johnson's Ferry Road, and cross the river.
5. Travel about one mile on Johnson's Ferry up the hill to a stoplight at Paper Mill Road at the top of the hill.
6. Turn left onto Paper Mill Road.
7. Proceed about two miles on Paper Mill Road to the trailhead parking on the left, soon after crossing Sope Creek on a bridge that was recently replaced and updated.

Activities

- Picnicking
- Fishing
- Family walks
- Hiking
- Fitness
- Trail running
- Wildlife observation

- Swimming
- Mountain biking
- Road biking

Trails

- An easy loop, fitness trail of about 3.5 miles suitable for everyone (easy)
- A loop through swamp and woods with several different routes of return (moderate)
- A system of mountain biking trails offering enthusiasts several alternatives (moderate for mountain bikers)
- A short loop through the woods for fitness enthusiasts (moderate)
- A long loop through the woods showcasing the best of the combined units (moderate to strenuous)
- A casual stroll of less than a mile around Sibley Pond (easy)
- A nice hike among the ruins of Sope Creek (moderate)

Please note that in this unit, the trails interconnect regularly; therefore, the possible hikes here are virtually limitless. An intrepid hiker can fashion almost any type of hike in this unit.

Unique Sights

- Many historical ruins (including the ruins of the Marietta Paper Mill, homesteads, and at least one historical cemetery)
- Large rock shelter with climbing routes
- Many routes for mountain biking
- Road biking along Columns Drive
- Sibley Pond
- Small waterfalls
- Sope Creek
- Decks for viewing the river
- Wildflowers
- Excellent wildlife-viewing opportunities

Facilities

- Picnic tables
- Grills
- Bathrooms accessible via Cochran Shoals and Columns Drive entrances
- Fitness trail
- Hiking trails
- Mountain biking trails
- Trash cans

The combined Cochran Shoals/Sope Creek Unit is a real treasure and may very well be the best unit in the entire CRNRA. Its southern reaches nearly touch I-285, yet it has some of the largest tracts of woods that a CRNRA hiker can hope to explore and provides incredible opportunities for viewing wildlife. There is something for everyone here. Vast woods, long trails, historical ruins, biking and trail-running opportunities, streams, and extensive wildlife grace this unit. I have long been a big fan of this unit because of the trail running and mountain biking found here, which I have come to enjoy on a weekly basis.

Recently, the National Park Service has engaged in an extensive program to change the trail system in the Cochran Shoals/Sope Creek Unit. Many of the older trails in this unit followed dirt access roads that led to homesteads and other features, and many of these roads/trails were constructed in a manner that permitted erosion during heavy rains. The Park Service recently solicited public opinion and found that many folks wanted more opportunities for mountain biking in the CRNRA. It then formulated a plan to extensively alter the trail system with the twofold objective to reduce erosion and impact on the land and to open up a larger and more remote trail system for mountain biking. The changes have been positive for the most part and have created additional opportunities for hiking, biking, and trail running. For me, the only downside has been the closing of some of my favorite trails, which required me to search for alternative trails that were not closed. In the end, it has been fun finding new places to explore.

The Cochran Shoals/Sope Creek Unit is easily the most popular unit in the CRNRA. Much of its popularity derives from the excellent fitness trail at the Cochran Shoals area, which runs about 3.5 miles in a flat lollipop loop of crushed gravel. The fitness trail provides an opportunity for trail running, biking, family walks, wildlife viewing, and river fishing. Runners flock to this trail, so much so that the parking lot overflows regularly, and it is often more of a people-watching opportunity than a wilderness experience. Although crowded, the fitness trail does provide excellent wildlife and nature-viewing opportunities, so don't miss it even if you like solitude more than crowds. This unit's popularity also stems from its other features, such as its extensive mountain biking trails, its remote network of hiking and running trails, its abundance of wildlife and historical ruins, and the easy access from three different points that lie accessible to much of Atlanta's population.

Regarding wildlife, I have had so many encounters with animals in this unit that it would be impossible to describe them all. However, I will describe a few such encounters to serve as examples. I have been trail running in the winter and come face-to-face with a coyote in the middle of the one remote trail in the Cochran Shoals Unit. I have nearly pushed a Baby Jogger over a large snake on the unit's fitness trail. I have come upon giant snapping turtles crawling across the same fitness trail and watched them from the nearby boardwalk while they swam underwater. I have been mesmerized by a barred owl staring at me from a tree twenty feet above my head, and I have watched a pileated woodpecker poke at a log on the ground fifteen feet in front of me. I have seen herons nest in the trees above the fitness trail. Among the animal species I have seen here are mallard ducks, great blue herons, red-tailed hawks, Canadian geese, marbled salamanders, toads, leopard frogs, black rat snakes, copperhead snakes, banded water snakes, fence swifts, brown skinks, fox, deer, beavers, muskrat, painted turtles, and the other species mentioned above. Songbirds are also plentiful in the spring. In the evening, the calls of barred owls ring out through the woods here.

I have been surprised at the number of deer that have recently come to populate this unit. Twenty or thirty years ago, an encounter with a deer was quite rare. Nowadays, it is not at all uncommon to see a deer along the fitness trail or along the more remote trails through the woods in this unit. In the fall, I have seen groups of three or more deer feeding along the fresh cut grass next to the fitness trail. In the summer, it is more likely to see deer back in the hills where the trails are more remote and the tree cover cooler.

Another nice aspect of this unit's trail system is the profusion of wildflowers, which becomes very evident to visitors who frequent the unit year-round. Different flowers bloom in the spring, summer, and fall. To find them, look along the stream bottoms and in open areas reached by the sun. Some flowers also frequent the swampy areas. Some of the more showy species are cardinal flower, catesby's trillium, toadshade trillium, aster, and trumpet creeper.

In short, I cannot find sufficient superlatives to adequately endorse this beautiful unit. Whether you are seeking a social experience, fitness, biking, fishing, or a wilderness visit, this unit has that for which you search. Beginners and wilderness veterans alike should visit this unit often. Few natural areas near Atlanta can match its appeal.

Trail Option 1
Cochran Shoals Fitness Trail Hike
(3.5 Miles Round-Trip—Easy)

Whenever Atlanta residents say that they are going down to the river for a walk or a run, they are probably referring to this scenic short trail. I have run, walked, and biked along this trail countless times, yet I still continue to see new and interesting sights here. Part of the allure is the plethora of interesting plants and animals that call this area home. Another benefit to this trail is that it is nearly flat, which makes for a leisurely run, walk, or bike ride. Bikes are, of course, allowed on this trail, and the wide crushed-gravel path is suitable for Baby Joggers, baby strollers, kids' bikes, and mountain bikes. In order to save your tires, I would recommend that you ride a mountain bike, rather than a road bike, on this trail. Road biking is better done along nearby Columns Drive.

This trail has evolved over the years that I have been coming here. At first, it was a normal, if wide, path frequented by nearby residents. Later, it became a fitness path, which was wider and more accessible. The Park Service then installed fitness stations where folks could do various exercises along the trail. It also constructed bathrooms near the midpoint of the trail, as well as benches, observation platforms, picnic tables, and wooden planters. Although some of these features remain today, the bathrooms have been moved to the two main trailheads at Cochran Shoals and Columns Drive, and the fitness equipment is nearly gone. Now the trail serves as a social gathering point for runners, friends, and families. It also serves as the central access point for the entire network of trails in this unit.

The trail can be accessed from the parking lot for the Cochran Shoals Unit on Interstate North Parkway, on the other side of the river from the Powers Island Unit. It can also be accessed from the alternate parking lot at the end of Columns Drive. This description of the trail will start at the gated entryway at the main parking lot off Interstate North Parkway. The trail itself is a lollipop loop with a head that is elongated into a large oval. The description will trace the loop in a counterclockwise fashion.

The entrance to the trail is marked by a large brown vehicle gate and trail kiosk where parking passes can be purchased with a credit card. The flat wide trail passes by several picnic tables and waste containers as it travels alongside the river. At about 0.1 miles, the actual trail loop begins with a low sign on the right indicating the start of the fitness loop. There is a nice observation platform on the river near this sign to the right. As you pass the Start sign, look to the left of the trail at the large rock outcrop overhanging the river floodplain. This rock outcrop contains a very difficult, overhanging rock climb called the Zipper, which should not be attempted without proper equipment and experience.

After the Start sign, you will note that similar low trail-marker posts inform trail users of the passing of each quarter mile. The posts marked in white give distances for the entire loop as described in this guide. The posts marked in yellow give distances for a shorter loop. This description will follow the white trail markers counterclockwise around the loop. Past the start, the trail continues to parallel the river that runs to the right of the trail. On the left side of the trail, you will begin to see the swampy, wet bogs that are characteristic of the floodplain in this area, which hide extensive wildlife. In wet weather and in the winter, these areas fill up with water to a high level, and water pours out of them and under the trail at several key points. Beavers are responsible for much of the water that is retained in these low-lying areas. If you observe the areas to the left of the trail closely, you will note several dam-style features created by beavers. It is also not uncommon to see trees gnawed by beavers near the base of the tree.

The wide trail meanders close to the river for its first quarter mile. Shortly after passing the quarter-mile post, look to the left to see the first of five access points into the trail network to the left (northwest) of the fitness trail. These access points will be discussed in more detail later in this chapter. You will immediately note that this access point is blocked by two newly installed inverted L-shaped signs that say "No bikes." Of the five access points along the fitness trail into the larger trail system, three are marked with these L-shaped signs to prevent bike riders from entering. The other two access points are the entrances to the new mountain bike loop and trail system and are, thus, not marked with such barriers.

In any event, you will note that past the barrier signs, this entrance to the trail network is actually a boardwalk over the bog that sits next to the fitness trail. This is a fine place to take a short stroll to observe wildlife such as turtles, beavers, and mallard ducks. One can also find numerous wildflowers in this area during certain times of the year.

Continuing along the fitness trail, you will pass an observation platform over the river on your right, just past the 0.5-mile marker. Take the opportunity to enjoy the sunshine and a good view of the river from this platform. There are usually some friendly ducks, geese, or herons to be seen. You may get a chance to see a fisherman or perhaps some kayakers or rafters.

Between 0.5 miles and 0.75 miles, you will note a grassy large area on your left, just before the trail crosses Sibley Creek via a stout bridge. In this grassy area, there used to be bathrooms; however, now the only thing remaining from the bathrooms is an old drinking fountain. Behind the grassy area is a weedy area, which used to be an activity field. It has become overgrown, and deer wander through this area to feed in the evenings.

As the trail crosses the stream, look down at the water to possibly observe some fish. There is a third observation deck on the banks of the river on the right-hand side, just after the bridge, which provides another chance to relax. Directly across the fitness trail from the third observation deck is a part of the fitness trail that parallels the creek upstream for about 0.25 miles. This short trail is a "cut through" that allows a hiker to access the rear portion of the lollipop loop. Unless you want a shorter stroll of one and one half miles, leave the "cut through" for your next hike or run.

Back on the main fitness trail, the next 0.75 miles are some of the most picturesque. The trail meanders through several areas along the river with large trees that overhang the trail and provide nice shade in the heat of the summer. In the fall, these areas provide beautiful color as the small leaves turn yellow and brown and then drift to the ground. In the spring, they are resplendent with their newly formed bright green leaves. Make sure to stay on the fitness trail through this area as another trail runs to the right and closer to the river here and rejoins the main trail.

Eventually, the trail reaches the far end of the loop and the alternate parking lot at the end of Columns Drive. This is a good place to take a break if you are trail running. There are bathrooms located in the parking lot, a drinking fountain, and a kiosk where parking passes can usually be purchased. There are also benches here for relaxing. The Columns Drive parking area is a good place to park if you want to run or ride a road bike along Columns Drive. The length of Columns Drive, from the parking lot to Johnson's Ferry Road, is about 2.5 miles and provides a nice flat run or road-bike ride through beautiful river estates and large houses. A golf course parallels the road (and the river) for a good portion of the ride too. I highly recommend Columns Drive for biking enthusiasts who want to improve their fitness by road biking or who want to enjoy a leisurely bike ride along the river.

Back on the fitness trail, the trail begins its journey through the rear portion of the lollipop loop. This part of the fitness trail is more exposed than the front part of the loop and, in the summer, receives a good deal of sun. It is also a great place to spot deer in the evenings, particularly in the fall and winter. The trail passes an access to the upper trail system on the right about 0.25 miles from the Columns Drive parking lot. This access is marked by the double L-shaped No Bikes signs. The trail then ascends a very small hill. This is the only hill on the fitness trail, and if you are not paying attention, you will miss it.

The trail then skirts along the area between the forest to the right of the trail and the floodplain to the left of the trail for about a half mile. Here you will find three more access points into the trail system and all the other trails discussed in this chapter. The first two of these access points occur just before the bridge spanning the same creek that you crossed earlier (Sibley Creek); neither of these is blockaded against bicycles. Instead, these access points provide mountain bikers the opportunity to ride into the hills on the loop described in more detail below. They are clearly marked with new signs designating the direction to ride based upon the day of the week. Don't miss the chance to stop atop the second bridge over Sibley Creek to look for snakes, fish, and beavers below.

The trail continues for another quarter mile in the same environment. During wet weather, water will trickle down through various chutes all along the back side of the fitness loop. Most of this water is channeled under the fitness trail through devious diversion pipes, but during the wet season, the trail in this area can occasionally fill with puddles of water.

Just before the trail turns sharply to the left to traverse through the boggy area beside the river, you will see the last access into the upper trail system, again barred with the characteristic new L-shaped signs. You will then see a marshy area, behind which there is a broad hill with a power cut across it. The viewpoint described in the next hike along Gumby Creek is at the top of the hill in the power cut in the distance. Look for ducks and beavers in this area. The trail then passes through a very interesting area—the often flooded, marshy bog separating the forest from the river. Look closely in this area for tadpoles, frogs, lizards, toads, ducks, and birds of many types. The cattails growing in this area are often beautiful as is the black-stained marsh water. In the fall, look for the flowers of orange (spotted) jewelweed and goldenrod throughout this area. The jewelweed attracts hummingbirds in the fall, so watch closely for them if the flower is blooming.

Soon, the loop portion of the trail ends near the second observation deck, and you can retrace your steps back to the trailhead. Enjoy your remaining journey. On this trail, you will have plenty of company in all but the worst weather conditions. You will likely see bike riders, dog walkers, strollers, Baby Joggers, trail runners, birders, photographers, trout fishermen, and sometimes, paddlers. Enjoy the company on this most popular of CRNRA trails, and visit often to see some of Atlanta's most fitness-oriented folks in a natural setting.

Trail Option 2
Nice Lollipop-Loop Hike through Ridge, Creek, and Marshy Terrain
(1.85 Miles—Moderate)

This trail provides hikers a great introduction to the wilder trails that can be found in the Cochran Shoals Unit. It provides access to a nice forested ridge, creek-side strolling, and interesting marshland floodplain. Wildflowers can be spotted here during the spring, and while on this trail, one can pretend that one is in a huge wilderness area because most of the hike has a very wild feel to it. Finally, this hike provides access to more challenging hikes along Gumby Creek.

The trail begins at the Interstate North Parkway trailhead for the fitness trail described above. From the gate at the entrance to the fitness trail, walk about 0.42 miles along the fitness trail (between fitness-trail mile markers for 0.25 miles and 0.5 miles), noting all the features described above. At 0.42 miles, you will see two inverted L-shaped signs barring bikes from a boardwalk area across the marshy riverside floodplain. Go between the two L-shaped signs, and begin walking down the boardwalk to continue this hike.

Take your time as you traverse the boardwalk. This is one of the best opportunities in the CRNRA to observe the wildlife and plant life that inhabit the floodplain alongside the river. Sometimes, the area under the boardwalk is flooded, but at other times, it is bone-dry. Either way, evidence of water is always close by in this area. If you look closely, you will see trees gnawed by beavers, as they build dams that cause this area to fill with water during wet seasons. Many flowers such as trumpet creeper and cardinal flower bloom in this area, along with honeysuckle and other sweet-smelling plants. In the fall, look for orange jewelweed growing alongside the boardwalk. These unique orange flowers hang down parallel to the ground and provide attraction for hummingbirds, which can be plentiful here when the flowers are blooming. Look for turtles in the water too, if there is water under the boardwalk. I once tracked a large snapping turtle through here as it swam under the boardwalk and crawled lazily along the bottom. Ducks are plentiful in this area too. A careful observer may see salamanders, lizards, frogs, and toads too.

At about 0.5 miles from the trailhead and about halfway down the boardwalk, you will encounter a wide sitting area with a couple of benches for relaxing. This is a wonderful place to linger, provided that it is not the mosquito season. Look for evidence of beaver activity here, including beaver dams causing pooling of creek water. This is a very moist and cool area of the trail.

Proceeding forward along the boardwalk, you will come to the end of the boardwalk section at about 0.53 miles from the trailhead. At this point, there is a signed intersection with a trail that comes in from the right-hand side of the trail, crossing a shallow creek as it does so. Take note of this trail because you may be returning this way, depending upon which of several return routes you take. In another short 0.02 miles, you will reach a second signed intersection, with a trail that comes in from uphill to the left. Near this signed intersection, you can find trillium flowers during the spring growing near the creek, including toadshade trillium (also known as spotted wake-robin) and catesby's trillium. Rather than proceeding straight ahead along the creek bottom, take the left-hand fork uphill at this signed intersection.

The trail will proceed uphill steeply at first and then bend to the right as it flattens out. Much of the trail up this hill has become eroded due to water cascading downhill in heavy rains, a testament to what happens when good trail-building practices are not employed. I would not be surprised if the National Park Service rerouted the trail in this area in the near future to avoid further erosion. Once you reach the top of the ridge at about 0.68 miles near a huge pine tree, you will enjoy a wonderful, though short, flat stroll of 0.3 miles through upland forest. As you walk through this area in the summertime, imagine you are hiking in the North Georgia Mountains. It is easy to do so as the solitude of the forest envelops you. It is difficult to believe that you are close to two major interstates and at least three other heavily traveled roads. You will enjoy this hike the most during the spring, summer, and fall. During winter, breaks in the trees reveal civilization close by.

At 0.93 miles, you will step out into a large open power cut, where you will immediately see a signed intersection. You can see many birds and flowers in this power cut during the main hiking seasons. In the late spring and summer, this area is a field of blooming asters, with thrashers, cardinals, and robins flitting between perches. If you turn left at this signed intersection, you will shortly come to a trailhead sign, two L-shaped No Bikes signs, and a trailhead at an office building complex. Intrepid explorers who wish to see more of the CRNRA trail system can pass through the two No Bikes signs and then take an immediate right turn on an indistinct trail across the power cut. This trail leads steeply downhill to the Gumby Creek trail system, which, if followed to its end, leads back to the fitness trail near a wildlife pond. If you would like more of a challenge, explore this area at your leisure.

Instead, this hike turns to the right upon entering the power cut at the signed intersection. The trail parallels the power cut, affording views down the cut and chances to observe flowers and, perhaps, some wildlife. At about one mile from the trailhead, the trail begins to dip downward, slowly at first and then steeply. At 1.15 miles, you will bottom out your descent temporarily and cross a small creek spilling out of a pipe to your right. Shortly thereafter, you will reach yet another signed trailhead, with a trail to the left and another proceeding straight ahead along the aforementioned creek. If you hike straight ahead, you will reenter the forest and follow the creek downhill back to the boardwalk at 1.32 miles from the trailhead. If you take this route, make sure to look for wildflowers along the creek in the spring, including trilliums. Once back at the boardwalk, you can retrace your steps about 0.55 miles back to the trailhead for a total hike of about 1.9 miles.

If, instead, you take the left-hand fork at the final signed trailhead, your journey will be only slightly longer. You will continue along the power cut uphill and then downhill to reach a dramatic overlook, where you can peer down from the power cut to the fitness trail and the wildlife pond below. Here you will find another signed intersection with a trail to the left, which leads again into the Gumby Creek portion of the CRNRA trail system. Head that way, if you are in the mood for further exploration.

Otherwise, head downhill on a sometimes eroded trail. Reenter the forest, and climb down past two large pine trees. Very shortly, you will reach the creek and a usually shallow stopover leading back to the first signed intersection and the aforementioned boardwalk, where you can retrace your earlier steps to the Interstate North trailhead. As you return along the boardwalk, you can appreciate how the work of beavers and the flat floodplain have changed the small creek that you stepped over into a broad marshy area suitable for birds and animals.

Trail Option 3
Unique "Mountain Biking Trail" Loop-Trail Experience with Optional Extension to Sibley Pond
(About Six Miles—Moderate)

Most of this trail was recently constructed by the National Park Service and its mountain biking partners and designed specifically for mountain bikes. Because the trail is designed for biking, I will limit this description to the major features of the trail. Please note that the entrances to this trail are clearly marked with large signs along the fitness-trail loop. As the signs clearly show, bikes are required to travel in certain directions based upon the day of the week. If you are biking, make sure to obey the directional signs, and do not exceed the speed limit because there are pedestrians along this trail who would not benefit from a collision with a mountain biker (neither would the bikers).

The easiest way to reach the mountain biking loop is to park at the Cochran Shoals parking area and take the fitness trail along the river. Stay to the right when the fitness trail forks at about 0.5 miles. Between 0.5

miles and 0.75 miles, the trail crosses over Sibley Creek on a stout bridge. At the far end of the bridge, turn left onto a spur of the fitness trail that parallels Sibley Creek upstream. In less than 0.25 miles, you will reach the first entrance to the mountain biking loop on the other side of the fitness trail. It will be marked by obvious signs. To reach the second entrance, do not go into the entrance along Sibley Creek. Instead, from the entrance sign, go right along the fitness trail for about 0.25 miles to the second entrance to the mountain biking loop, which is also marked clearly with trail signs. Neither entrance is barred by L-shaped No Bikes signs.

Proceeding from the first (Sibley Creek) entrance, the mountain biking loop follows along Sibley Creek upstream through some very muddy areas and then through a very rocky area. You will note two small cascades in the stream beside you, which can be pretty, depending upon water flow. You will also note that you are paralleling a sewer connection as the manholes are occasionally visible.

At about 0.35 miles from the Sibley Creek entrance, the trail will reach a large sewer manhole in the middle of the trail next to the creek. Three trails lead off from this intersection. One bends sharply to the right and uphill but is barred by No Bikes signs. Another crosses the creek straight ahead. The third is the trail you want to take if you are riding a mountain bike. It bends to the right around the manhole cover, passes a trail sign, and begins a gradual ascent through the woods in a secluded creek valley. This section of the trail was recently constructed. It meanders back and forth through various wooded valleys for over a mile. It is a beautiful trail in the spring or fall, but it is a long jaunt for walking because of the many meanders.

Enjoy riding the trail through this remote and pristine portion of the CRNRA. You will be enchanted by the forest in this area during certain times of the year. After nearly two miles of riding, you will arrive at an area that I like to call the Balcony, because it is near the top of a ridge and has many trails leading off from it. As you initially reach the Balcony, you will see two L-shaped signs saying "No bikes" immediately on your right. Bend to your left away from these signs, and you will see another trail on your left leading to some houses. Do not take this trail, but instead, turn gradually to your right.

Just past a wood fence (if it has not been removed by the Park Service), you will see a third trail leading off to your left and downhill about twenty yards from the trail leading to the houses. You may take this trail if you want a longer ride. It leads into the Sope Creek Unit and the remainder of the mountain biking trail system. It can be a fun ride for experienced riders as it winds its way down, then up, then down again to Sibley Pond and the trailhead at Sope Creek. This is also the longer trail detailed below for hiking or trail running. If you hike or run in this direction, beware of mountain bikers, particularly on the narrower sections of trail.

Assuming you do not take this left-hand turn into the remainder of the mountain biking trail system, you will continue straight ahead onto an old roadbed that was obviously graded to be level. In less than 0.2 miles, you will reach a turn to the right to continue the mountain biking loop. The turn is currently well marked with a sign for the mountain bike loop, but if you end up behind some apartments, you have missed the turn by about 0.15 miles. Take this turn to the right, and descend for about one mile. Once the trail has finished descending on a fast and well-graded downhill path, it reaches a usually dry creek bottom and climbs a short hill to an intersection. Proceed straight through the four-way intersection as the two other paths are marked by the usual No Bikes signs.

The trail will initially remain level and then begin ascending after crossing a short wooden bridge. The ascent is generally moderate, although it becomes somewhat steep just before it reaches a signed T intersection near the top of the hill. At this intersection, turn left, and proceed on a fast, fun long downhill back down to the fitness trail at the second entrance to the mountain biking trail system. Turn right on the fitness trail, and follow it back to the parking lot at Cochran Shoals. This is an exhilarating ride on a moderate-trail loop that will enchant nature lovers and provide veteran riders with a challenge. Because of its charms and its location, it can be crowded, so make sure to keep an eye out for fellow riders and walkers.

Trail Option 4
Short Loop through the Woods
for Trail Runners and Fitness Enthusiasts
(4.5 Miles—Moderate)

This is perhaps one of the finest hikes in the Cochran Shoals Unit. I simply love this loop as a trail run, and I have run and hiked it hundreds of times. It is just long enough to give one a good challenge and a nice taste of nature yet short enough to be completed in an hour and twenty minutes of running or a couple of hours of steady hiking. It passes by a creek and through beautiful forest. It has also been, for me, a great place to spot wildlife, particularly in the spring. This hike incorporates portions of other hikes described in this chapter but is a great outing all in its own. Enjoy it whenever you get a chance.

The hike starts behind the gate at the beginning of the fitness trail at the Cochran Shoals parking lot. It proceeds along the fitness trail under the tree canopy along the river to the split in the fitness trail at about 0.46 miles. You can take either fork; however, I usually take the right fork along the river. Look for some stately large pine trees on the right-hand side at about 0.53 miles. At about 0.6 miles, you will cross Sibley Creek on a concrete bridge. Look for fish in the creek water below.

Turn left along the fitness-trail connector trail immediately after crossing the creek bridge. This wide connector trail zigzags under a nice, shaded tree canopy growing in the river floodplain. At about 0.76 miles, you will reach the start of the mountain bike trail straight ahead as you cross the fitness trail. If you take the left fork at the split in the fitness trail, you will arrive at the same location after crossing the creek bridge located at the start of the mountain bike trail. Proceed straight ahead onto the mountain bike trail that parallels Sibley Creek, which runs along the left-hand side of the trail.

Proceed through several muddy areas. These muddy bogs became worse after the trail became designated for mountain bike riding. In some instances, the only way to deal with the bogs is to creep along the sides or to rock-hop through the middle of the mud. Be patient because the trail quality will improve for the rest of the hike/run, although it turns very rocky before it flattens out later. At 0.99 miles, you will note a nice waterslide in the creek on your left. This is a good place to take a break. At 1.05 miles, you will reach a convergence of four trails at a prominent sewer manhole in the middle of the trail at a clearing.

At this point you should take a hard right turn uphill and begin an ascent up an old road grade, almost immediately crossing the newly constructed mountain bike trail through two sets of "L" shaped "No Bikes" signs. Do not take the trail that crosses the creek, and do not follow the mountain bike loop past the CRNRA sign. This uphill portion of the trail can be rocky as it picks its way up to the top of the hill that looks down onto the river in this area. The uphill can be strenuous, but it is short as you reach the top of the grade at 1.32 miles. Make sure to check out the mature forest as you ascend the hill. The oaks in this area are beautiful as their new green leaves sprout in the spring and when their colorful leaves drop in the fall.

At the top of the hill, you will begin a rolling journey along the top of the ridgeline of the hill on an old roadbed. At 1.36 miles, you will pass a wooden fence on your right (if the NPS has left it standing), and at 1.42 miles, you will pass a trail coming in from the right at a signed intersection. Do not take this trail that descends rapidly back down to the fitness trail. Instead, proceed along the old roadbed that rides the crest of the hill, enjoying the beauty of the forest. While running on this portion of the trail, I once ran face-to-face into a coyote.

At 1.58 and 1.60 miles, you will see signed trail intersections with trails leading off to the right. These trails lead a very short distance to an old family cemetery tucked away in the woods, of which most folks using the CRNRA are unaware. It is definitely worth a visit as its historic value is undeniable. It is surrounded by an old metal fence that is disintegrating with age. There is a separate fenced grave of a mother who lived from 1826 to 1882. There is also a large monument to the Scribner family, dating from 1863 to 1883. Looking at this cemetery, one can get a sense of how difficult pioneer life in this area must have been. The side trail to the cemetery is about 0.1 miles long. It also connects at a newly signed intersection to a trail leading downhill to the fitness trail. If you take this trail downhill, don't miss the huge oak tree on the right-hand side of the trail with a tunnel going all the way through the lower trunk of the tree!

Back on the main trail, you will continue your rolling hike along the ridgetop until you reach a signed intersection on the right for a cutoff spur at 1.71 miles. Immediately thereafter, at 1.75 miles, you will drop down over some rocks and through two No Bikes signs to an area I like to call the Balcony, where multiple trails converge. The mountain bike trail connects on the left immediately after the No Bikes signs, and there is also a trail to the left leading into some houses. Avoid both of these turnoffs, and bend to the right and straight ahead, following the old roadbed.

Just after passing the two turnoffs described above, you will reach a third trail intersection on your left, just after a wooden fence (if the fence is still in place). This turn to the left is the extension of the mountain biking trail that leads into the remaining trail system and the Sope Creek Unit area. The next hike in this book describes a route that includes this trail system. However, on this shorter hike, avoid this turnoff, and continue on the old roadbed straight ahead, passing another turnoff spur on the right. At 1.88 miles, you will reach an intersection with a trail leading downward on the right. Proceeding straight ahead at this intersection will lead you into some apartment buildings within one hundred yards or so. This intersection is clearly marked with signs for the mountain biking loop. Take this right-hand turn, and proceed downhill.

For some unknown reason, the graded portion of the trail between the Balcony and the turnoff to the right onto the mountain biking trail has always been a place where I have spotted unusual wildlife. For instance, as I was traversing this section on a recent run, I startled a bat that was on the ground near my feet, and it flew up past my head on its journey to the skies. On another occasion, I came upon a large black rat snake stretched across the trail and coaxed it to one side of the trail so that I could pass. I also once happened upon a pileated woodpecker in this section that was on the ground, pecking at a piece of wood. I stood and watched the bird for five minutes until it became frustrated and flew away. On yet another trip, I happened to see a barred owl on a tree branch about ten feet above the trail in this section. Again, I stopped and watched the bird for a few minutes before proceeding. I have also encountered other wildlife here, such as turtles, frogs, toads, birds, and salamanders.

After taking the right turn onto the mountain biking trail, the path undulates back and forth as it descends toward the river. Keep your eyes and ears open for mountain bikers in this section of trail. They often speed downhill to take advantage of the well-graded trail. This section of trail was created recently for mountain bikers, and it is easy to see the influence bikers had on the construction of the trail. It loops back and forth and takes its leisurely time in reaching the level of the river floodplain. As you hike, keep your eyes open for wildlife, and observe the beautiful, mostly hardwood forest through which this trail passes.

At 2.49 miles, you will cross a small wooden bridge over a drainage, and then at 2.51 miles, you will reach the bottom level of the trail. After you reach the bottom in a muddy area, you will ascend briefly to a four-way intersection at 2.56 miles. The trail straight ahead is the mountain bike trail. The trail to your right passes uphill through two L-shaped No Bikes signs and winds its way up to the cemetery that you may have visited earlier in your hike. Do not take either of these two options. Instead, proceed downhill to the left through two No Bikes signs for a short stretch to intersect with the broad gravel fitness trail. Here, make a right onto the fitness trail, and travel back to the trailhead at Cochran Shoals.

When you reach the fitness trail, you will be about 1.5 miles from the trailhead at Cochran Shoals. Enjoy the warm sunshine afforded by the wide-open fitness trail. About 0.5 miles from the turnoff onto the fitness trail, you will reach the signed intersection for the entrance to the mountain biking trail along Sibley Creek and the bridge over Sibley Creek. To vary your hike, proceed straight ahead, rather than to the left, to reach the trailhead on the fitness trail's right-hand fork. By the time you reach the trailhead at about 4.5 miles, you will be ready for a good meal and a drink. Enjoy this hike whenever you have two or more hours of freedom and the desire to commune with nature!

Trail Option 5
Long Loop through the Woods
Showcasing the Best of the Combined Units
(Six Miles—Moderate to Strenuous)

This hike showcases all the best of the Cochran Shoals and Sope Creek Units and can be considered to be the ultimate "tour de Cochran/Sope." It includes many of the sights and historic areas in the other hikes found in this chapter but also exposes you to more deep woods, creeks, and wild areas. This is an ideal trail run and is often used by local high school and college cross-country teams for training. You will want to stop often on this hike/run and look at wildlife and forest. If you trail run this loop, give yourself at least two hours and fifteen minutes to complete it. If you hike it, you will need four hours or so to complete the loop for an average-to-slow hiker. Don't miss this one in the spring or fall for a great taste of nature close to home!

This hike begins the same way as trail option 4 for the first 1.75 miles. Begin at the Cochran Shoals parking lot, and follow the fitness trail about 0.76 miles to the start of the mountain biking trail along Sibley Creek. Follow the mountain biking trail along Sibley Creek to the sewer manhole cover marking the intersection of four trails. Take the same hard right turn between the L-shaped No Bikes signs, as described in trail option 4, and climb to the top of the small ridge. Roll along the top of the ridge in the same manner as trail option 4, stopping, if you like, to visit the old cemetery, until you reach the Balcony at 1.75 miles. Here the mountain biking trail enters on the left as you pass through the No Bikes blockade, and a second trail to the left leads to some houses. Proceed down and to the right along the old road grade, bypassing these two trail options to the left. After passing a wooden fence (assuming it has not been removed) a few yards later, you should see a third trail leading off to the left. This is the entrance to the remainder of the mountain biking trail system and the path that you should take to continue this long-loop hike through the forest.

Here the true nature fun begins as you will enjoy a 2.5-mile loop through extensive woods before returning to this point. Initially, the trail descends through some switchbacks designed to retard the erosion process. The trail descends to a low point where Fox Creek crosses underneath the trail via a culvert at 1.91 miles. In the summertime, Fox Creek barely flows, but in the spring, there is a substantial stream flowing in the creek bed. After crossing the creek, the trail immediately bends to the right, away from an old roadbed that the National Park Service is trying to reclaim from erosion. The trail then parallels the creek until it reaches a signed intersection with a trail entering from the left at 1.98 miles. This trail is the mountain biking trail, and all bikes must turn to the left here. However, if you are hiking or running, proceed straight ahead at this signed intersection, secure in the knowledge that on your return trip, you will arrive from this left side on the mountain bike trail.

For the next quarter mile, the trail drops gradually down along Fox Creek, which runs on the right-hand side of the trail. In the winter, you will notice apartment buildings far above on the other side of the creek, but in the other seasons, the tree leaves make the buildings invisible, giving a hiker the sense of wilderness. At 2.21 miles from the trailhead, you will cross a small wooden bridge over a rivulet coming down from the hill, which is a tributary of Fox Creek. There is a signed intersection with a side trail here that has No Bikes signs guarding it. The trail then rises and continues its flat parallel of Fox Creek. Many flowers grow in this area in the spring. Especially prevalent are toadshade trillium and catesby's trillium.

At 2.35 miles from the trailhead, you will begin a short uphill climb, which culminates at a wooden fence (or other blockade) blocking further travel on the old roadbed. Here, at 2.39 miles, the trail bends sharply to the right and descends steeply to a wooden bridge built in 2007 by Boy Scout Troop 795. The bridge crosses another small tributary of Fox Creek, and on the other side of the bridge, you will be faced with a T intersection and some apartment buildings. Going right at the T will lead you into the apartments. Therefore, turn left, and follow the trail uphill as it parallels the rear of the apartment buildings. After about one-tenth of a mile, you will reach an intersection with another trail on the left, which will have the usual No Bikes sign blockades, with which you should be familiar by now. The apartments will still be visible to your right.

Proceeding straight ahead will lead you into the Sope Creek Unit and, perhaps, down to Sope Creek, depending upon which trails you take. Save this hike for another day as it can be beautiful and interesting. Take note of the mountain laurel bushes that grow in this area.

Rather than proceeding forward, take the trail to your left, and go through the L-shaped blockades. You will go up a moderately steep uphill grade, and then the trail will flatten out again. You will note that this trail again follows an old roadbed. After about 0.2 miles from the last intersection, you will hit another intersection with a trail forking to the right toward the Sope Creek trail system. Proceed to the left and straight ahead, rather than turning right, and you will again go through two No Bikes signs. You will still be on a wide rocky old roadbed.

At about 2.75 miles from the trailhead and about 0.25 miles from the left turn away from the apartment buildings, you will see another trail coming in from the left through No Bikes signs at a signed intersection. Proceed straight ahead, and keep your eyes peeled for an old cabin chimney and foundation on your right. The old homestead chimney still stands proudly in the woods while the remains of the cabin are nearly gone. If you look closely, you will see some remains of the building's foundation. This is an interesting place to linger and explore, but please do not disturb any of the historical remains. Allow others to find them just as you did.

About 0.1 miles past the old chimney, you will reach yet another signed T intersection with a wide path. This is the mountain biking trail from which you departed a while back. If you want to extend your hike, turn to the right, and proceed about 0.5 miles to Sibley Pond. You can circle the pond on a nice trail and then return the way you came. You can also access the entire Sope Creek trail system from Sibley Pond.

However, for purposes of this hike, turn left on the mountain bike trail at about 2.8 miles from the trailhead, and follow the wide path. Beware of bikers traveling this trail rapidly in either direction. In this area, you will note many pine trees and often hear the loud pecking of woodpeckers of various species. At about 3.0 miles from the trailhead, there will be a signed trail leading off to the left through No Bikes signs. This trail cuts through the woods in the middle of the loop that you are hiking. If you want to observe some nice forest, take this side trail on another hike. A few steps later, there will be a signed trail leading to the right with No Bikes signs. This trail leads back down to Sibley Pond and its inlet stream. This is another nice trail to take when you have more time. About 0.02 miles later, you will see another trail leading off to the right. This trail is closed and appears to lead out of the CRNRA.

Continue on the old roadbed/mountain bike trail through beautiful forest. This area of the hike is unparalleled in the Atlanta area for solitude and a sense of wilderness. Only the mountain bikers and other hikers will make you feel as if you are near a big city. On the return trip, you will note that the National Park Service has blockaded the old roadbed at certain points and forced trail users to take newly carved mountain bike trail. The trail rejoins the old roadbed occasionally, only to be pushed again onto newer track cut for mountain bikers. It appears that this construction was accomplished in order to avoid further erosion.

At 3.11 miles from the trailhead, you will see another signed trail coming in from the left through No Bikes signs. Do not take this trail as it leads across the loop to trail that you have already hiked. Shortly after this intersection, look for a large magnolia tree on the left-hand side of the trail. If you are hiking in the winter, magnolias are easy to spot because they are some of the few trees that hold green leaves during winter. You will note that holly bushes and pines are the other main greenery to be found in this forest during the winter.

At around 3.41 miles from the trailhead, the trail bends away to the left from the old roadbed and begins a winding descent on switchbacks. The trail in this area is narrow, and one should keep watch for mountain bikers who are traveling rapidly down this narrow descent. At 3.6 miles from the trailhead, you will reach the T intersection with the loop trail where you proceeded straight ahead earlier in your hike. Turn right on the level path; cross Fox Creek on the same culvert as before, and ascend the switchbacks of the mountain biking trail to the Balcony at nearly four miles. From here, retrace your steps to the right along the ridge, down along Sibley Creek, and back along the fitness trail to the Cochran Shoals trailhead at nearly six miles. If you want to vary your hike further, turn left when you reach the Balcony, and follow the trail instructions for trail option 4 down to the fitness trail.

There are few, if any, hikes so near to Atlanta that give a hiker as much of a wilderness feeling as this one. I hope you enjoy it.

Trail Option 6
Casual Short Stroll around Sibley Pond
for Families with Young Children
(0.47 Miles—Easy)

The Sibley Pond loop provides a great opportunity for families to take a stroll together, even with toddlers. It's a flat trail that gives kids the opportunity to experience the outdoors without working too hard or committing to a long walk. Plus, the walk provides an opportunity for fishing with youngsters.

The walk begins behind the forest service gate at the Sope Creek Unit trailhead. The Sope Creek trailhead provides picnic tables for those who want to have a picnic meal in the woods, as well as parking, and perhaps, garbage receptacles. To the right of the picnic tables is the brown forest service gate, behind which the wide gravel trail begins. This wide trail, which initially resembles more of a service road, provides access to much of the CRNRA trail system in this area. Initially, it travels gradually downhill toward Sibley Pond. Mountain bikers are allowed on this section of trail, so watch out for them.

At about 0.07 miles down the trail, the first signed trail junction is reached as a connector to the historic mill ruins runs off to the left, and access to the pond loop in a counterclockwise fashion is to the right. Proceed straight ahead, toward the dam of the pond, as this hike description follows the shoreline in a clockwise manner. You will pass another short access to the back of the loop on your right at another signed intersection just as you reach the open dam of the pond at 0.09 miles.

Take your time crossing the dam. This is a wonderful area to observe birds and wildflowers in the spring and to feel the rays of the sun on your skin after a long winter. After a short way, you will see a small dock extending out into the pond near its outflow stream. This dock is a great place to observe the small fish, including largemouth bass and bream that inhabit the pond. Every now and again, the fish will swim by, giving the kids something to talk about and the grown-ups a reason to wish they had brought their fishing poles. If you decide to fish, make sure you are properly licensed and observing all fishing regulations.

At 0.13 miles, you will cross the outlet stream, and you will see the wide mountain biking and hiking trail leading off to the left shortly thereafter. This trail leads deep into the area's trail system and is described in more detail above. The pond hike leads to the right, reaches a mound, and then proceeds through the woods alongside the pond. Bikes are not allowed on this portion of the level trail, which gives the hiker many nice views of the pond through the forest and shoreline plants.

At 0.27 miles, hikers will reach a wooden bridge over the inlet creek, quickly followed by a signed intersection with a trail leading on a loop to the left through the woods. This small-loop trail initially parallels the inlet creek and gives a hiker the chance to explore the surrounding woods. It then intersects the pond loop again shortly ahead at a signed intersection on the left. Rather than take the left turn, the hiker on the pond loop will go straight and will immediately cross a second bridge over the pond's inlet and will continue following the shoreline of the pond. At 0.35 miles, you will reach a nice log lying in the pond where turtles of many sorts can usually be observed sunning themselves.

At 0.37 miles, you will reach the pond dam and the end of the loop beside an L-shaped No Bikes sign and another sign describing the life of a pond. Here you should turn left and go shortly uphill on the lead in gravel trail to the trailhead at 0.47 miles. Alternatively, expand your hike by visiting the Sope Creek ruins or by walking some of the mountain biking trail toward the Cochran Shoals Unit. The hike around Sibley Pond provides a nice stroll for families and a great introduction to the wonders of the CRNRA.

Trail Option 7
Short Walk Down to View Historic Ruins of a Paper Mill
(0.9 Miles—Easy)

History buffs will find this hike hard to beat. Between 1855 and 1902, the Marietta Paper Mill produced paper at the mill on the banks of Sope Creek, near the trailhead for the Sope Creek Unit. In 1864, Union troops burned the original mill. The mill was rebuilt after the Civil War, and the ruins that stand there today are what remain from these rebuilding efforts. They provide a fascinating opportunity for exploration. Comparing these ruins to the others described in this book gives the hiker a brilliant vision of life as it was long ago, when Atlanta was less populated. This hike is an easy one, to be enjoyed by folks of all ages who are physically fit enough to hike sloped trails. Enjoy it, but be sure to leave the ruins and all artifacts exactly as you found them.

Begin this hike behind the picnic tables at the Sope Creek Unit trailhead. Although the ruins can also be accessed by going down the trail behind the large gate, this description will follow the trail through the woods from the picnic tables. Initially, the hiker will go through two L-shaped No Bikes signs and descend gradually through the woods. Enjoy the forest as you anticipate the historic ruins to be found ahead.

At 0.09 miles, you will reach a signed trail junction. Go left here as the right-hand fork goes back toward the main trail and the Sibley Pond area. A farther walk through the forest brings the hiker to another signed trail junction at 0.18 miles. Go left here. Going to the right will lead a hiker deeper into the Sope Creek/Cochran Shoals trail system. While exploring this right-hand branch trail, the author found himself traversing some nice forest toward the Cochran Shoals Unit and, at one point, found himself down along the banks of rushing Sope Creek.

After turning to the left at 0.18 miles, the trail will nearly reach Paper Mill Road before sharply switching back to the right at 0.23 miles. The trail then parallels the road downhill, steeply at times, toward the historic ruins. At 0.39 miles, you will face another trail intersection. A right turn here will lead you back up the hillside where there is a blue blaze on a tree, whereas a left turn goes steeply down toward the road. I recommend going downhill to the left here as the quicker way to access the ruins. At 0.44 miles, you will reach the ruins along Sope Creek as you parallel the road and a small creek that runs along the road.

Take your time exploring here. You will note that many folks choose to sunbathe on the rocks in Sope Creek. The Paper Mill Road bridge was recently replaced with a sturdier and modern bridge, so you can admire the handiwork of the bridge crews while looking over the historical ruins. Even with the new bridge, it cannot be questioned that this is a place of uncommon beauty. The ruins of the mill stretch towerlike toward the sky above you as you walk along the creek. Take note of the fact that on the other side of the creek, there is a rock wall that appears to have been built during the same historic time as the mill. There are also other mill ruins on the far side of the creek, downstream of Paper Mill Road. For intrepid explorers, the creek is shallow enough to cross at many points in order to explore the ruins on the far side. The main building of the old paper mill is the largest stone building ruin along Sope Creek. It is located on the eastern side of the creek, at the point where a small rocky stream flows into Sope Creek from its eastern side. The ruins on the eastern side of the creek are difficult to access because of the lack of any true trail. Explore at your own option and your own risk.

As you explore this area, remind yourself of the history. Union troops serving under Gen. Kenner Garrard burned the original mill on July 8, 1864, in part because it produced high-quality paper for Confederate currency. After the war, the mill was rebuilt and began to supply newsprint paper for local newspapers. The company changed ownership in the late 1890s, and the mill closed in 1903, perhaps because of a newly opened mill nearby that was powered by electricity rather than water. The ruins have been vacant for about a century; however, the Forest Service has stabilized the ruins and cared for them in recent years. Hikers should respect the efforts put into these ruins by the government and leave them as they are for others to enjoy.

Return to the trailhead as you came. The total hike, from the trailhead to the first set of ruins along the road and back, is about 0.9 miles. This hike is another unique one in the CRNRA and should be included in any list of the best hikes in the CRNRA.

Sidebar 1
Trail Running

The Cochran Shoals/Sope Creek Unit is another place in the CRNRA that is near and dear to me. Throughout my adult life, I have made use of this unit as my favorite area to recreate. The most important aspect of my travels here has been trail running. Trail running has increased greatly in popularity since 1980 and often finds its home in places like the Cochran Shoals Unit of the CRNRA. The trails in this unit interconnect so well that a trail runner has virtually unlimited options for training in the woods. The woods provide shade to trail runners like myself, who like to enjoy running out of the blistering Atlanta summer heat. Mosquitoes are not a problem for trail runners who rarely stand still long enough to be attacked.

Trail runners enjoy several benefits over folks who run primarily on pavement. One of those advantages is the ability to see and enjoy nature. Another advantage is better conditioning of foot muscles due to the uneven tread of the trail, which must be negotiated. A third advantage to trail running is that a trail runner concentrates on foot placement and natural surroundings and, thus, is less aware of any pain or exhaustion from running. Finally, trail runners usually do not have to worry about getting run over by cars!

Two of my most favorite trail-running routes are chronicled in this chapter. If you decide to trail run, watch your step as it is very easy to trip on roots or rocks. Take water and/or energy gels with you to keep your body running at peak capacity. Also, please take a cell phone or other emergency contact device with you. Many of the trails in this area are remote, and it would be long before you were found if you suffered a medical emergency. Enjoy these trails with a healthy respect for their wild character, and you will have many years of good running.

Sidebar 2
Sope Creek

There are two theories as to where the name of Sope Creek originated. One theory holds that the creek is named after an old Cherokee chief named Sope, who remained in the area long after others left and who was friendly to children. The other theory is that the name comes from an early-1800 soap mill on the creek. Read the literature, and decide for yourself which is most plausible. In either event, the creek itself is a beautiful one for the piedmont area, filled with rocks and rushing rapids that are not normally characteristic of the area. Sope Creek reaches its final destination at the banks of the Chattahoochee along Columns Drive in a peaceful setting where fish and birds dwell. Thus, one can observe the rocky creek upstream in the forest near the mill ruins or at its placid end along Columns Drive near the back entrance to the Cochran Shoals Unit.

The entrance to the fitness trail is a popular place.

The fitness trail is wide and well maintained.

The fitness trail has mile markers every quarter mile.

The entrance to the boardwalk area on the fitness trail includes signs prohibiting bikes.

The boardwalk travels through wetlands along the fitness trail.

This overlook in the Cochran Shoals Unit gives a view of the fitness trail and nearby wetlands.

Wildflowers can easily be found in the Cochran Shoals Unit.

Signs such as this one direct mountain bikers on the mountain bike trail in the Cochran Shoals Unit.

Trumpet Creeper is one of the common wildflowers in the Cochran Shoals Unit.

The ruins on Sope Creek are beautiful at twilight.

The trail in the Sope Creek Unit crosses the dam at Sibley Pond.

Sibley Pond is a great place to relax and spot wildlife.

Sope Creek runs along the edge of the Sope Creek Unit into the Chattahoochee River.

The masonry in the Sope Creek ruins is interesting.

The Sope Creek ruins are definitely worth exploring.

Make sure to closely observe the construction of the masonry windows in the Sope Creek ruins.

Signs such as this one guide hikers, bikers, and runners in the Sope Creek Unit trail system.

Signs such as these guide bikers away from the hiking-only trails in the Sope Creek Unit.

Nice wide trails like this one can be found in the Sope Creek Unit.

Fall colors can be very beautiful in the Sope Creek Unit

Signs such as this one guide mountain bikers in the Cochran Shoals/Sope Creek Unit.

This old homestead chimney stands beside the trails in the Sope Creek Unit.

Closer inspection of the old chimney in the Sope Creek Unit reveals interesting details.

CHAPTER 6

THE JOHNSON'S FERRY SOUTH UNIT - WILDLIFE ABOUNDS HERE

Directions to the Johnson's Ferry South Unit

1. Take I-285 east to Exit 24 (Riverside Drive).
2. Turn left onto Riverside Drive, and cross the bridge over I-285.
3. Travel about 2.2 miles north on Riverside Drive until you reach the stoplight at Johnson's Ferry Road, after a steep downhill curve.
4. Turn left onto Johnson's Ferry Road, and travel 0.25 miles, crossing the river. Immediately after the river is a stoplight at Columns Drive.
5. Turn left onto Columns Drive, and proceed about 1 mile to the parking area and trailhead on the left.
6. From I-285 west, take Exit 24, and turn right onto Riverside Drive.
7. Follow the same directions above.

Activities

- Picnicking
- Fishing
- Family walks
- Hiking
- Trail running
- Wildlife observation

Trails

- An easy, out-and-back stroll along the river of about 0.5 miles with the chance to see wildlife (easy)

Unique Sights

- The river
- Many chances to see wildlife

Facilities

- Pavilion
- Trails
- Trash cans

Consisting of about seventy acres of floodplain and open spaces between Columns Drive and the river, the Johnson's Ferry South Unit is small but provides a perfect getaway for those who want to experience nature without working too hard. It includes just one trail of about one half mile in length that runs along the river within sight of the slow-moving waters. When visiting this unit, I almost always see animals. Rabbits are ubiquitous, and hawks and owls ply their trades in this area too. I have also seen snakes, lizards, many birds, and other critters when hiking here. The trail in this unit is not open for bicycles, but it is a good trail to bring a dog for a nice little walk, perhaps in the evening after work.

One interesting aspect of this unit is the old pavilion in the field behind the forest service gate on the right-hand side of the trailhead. It looks like a really nice place to have a picnic, but before you attempt to use it, you should probably contact the headquarters of the CRNRA to find out whether the National Park Service allows visitors to use the pavilion and, if so, under what terms.

The Johnson's Ferry Units preserve the area around where William Johnson operated a ferry from the 1850s until 1879. Mr. Johnson carried travelers across the river on his ferry, before the modern bridges made things more accessible for those wishing to cross the wide Chattahoochee River.

The Johnson's Ferry South Unit is easily accessible, is infrequently visited, and provides a lot of nature for very little effort. Enjoy it.

Trail Option 1
River Hike
(1.0 Miles Out and Back—Easy)

This short hike is the only one found in the Johnson's Ferry South Unit, but it is worth visiting. It starts behind the large rocks blocking vehicles from entering the trail just off the parking lot and near the CRNRA trailhead signs. It provides a nice stroll of an hour or less along the riverbank.

When visiting the Johnson's Ferry South Unit, you will first note that trails proceed both to the left and to the right behind the vehicle-blocking rocks. Investigation will show that the trail to the right peters out very quickly along the riverbank. However, there is another unofficial trail that starts behind the metal gate on the right-hand side. This trail leads immediately to an open, grassy field with a large pavilion in the middle. Following the trail leads one back into the woods for about 0.3 miles, and ultimately, the path ends at a post deep in the woods. The author found this floodplain forest area to be very buggy in the summer and probably not worth visiting, unless one has a yen for exploration.

The main trail is more obvious, consisting of a broad sandy path leading to the left along the river behind the large rocks bordering the parking area. The Park Service appears to clear this trail, providing a good view of wildlife on the trail ahead. Often, one can see rabbits feeding on the trailside grass ahead or squirrels and birds flitting about. Approach them with care to ensure the best view before they escape into the underbrush. I have observed many robins and brown thrashers when hiking along this trail. I have also seen brown skinks and five-lined skinks here in the spring. In the evening, a sighting of a deer or fox is not out of the question.

The trail is very quiet and secluded, and there is very little, if any, elevation change. It has a very sylvan and shaded feel that is appealing to casual hikers. At about 0.3 miles down the trail, you will note some water on the left during wet-weather seasons. As the trail nears its end, it bends to the left to reach what used to be another parking area behind a gate, which is now overgrown. In this area, there are often brown rabbits feeding on the grass. This area used to have fields where athletic teams would play polo, lacrosse, and soccer back in the 1970s. However, the Park Service has allowed all this area to become wild and overgrown. The trail ends after just over 0.5 miles, and the hiker then has to retrace his or her steps back to the trailhead. All in all, this trail provides a very relaxing and enjoyable experience to the casual hiker.

Sidebar 1
Columns Drive

One of the recreation spots I have long enjoyed is Columns Drive. Columns Drive borders the Johnson's Ferry South Unit all along its side farthest away from the river, and at its far end is the parking lot for the Cochran Shoals Unit. It provides a nice flat 2.5-mile run or bike ride for athletes of all stripes. I have spent many long hours biking this road, which is particularly beautiful in the spring. There are flowers and beautiful homes to capture your attention when biking here. If you decide to bike or run on Columns Drive, please make sure to abide by the signed regulations. There have been some political disputes about how Columns Drive is used, and bikers and runners ultimately won the debate. However, you can ensure that this fine road will remain open for running and bike riding by abiding by the laws and regulations that are clearly marked along the road.

The trailhead for the Johnson's Ferry South Unit contains the usual trail and parking signs.

The trail in the Johnson's Ferry South Unit is wide and follows the riverbank.

This gate, and the pavillion beyond, are to the right of the trailhead in the Johnson's Ferry South Unit.

This pavillion resides in a field south of the parking area in the Johnson's Ferry South Unit.

The wide trail in the Johnson's Ferry South Unit can be alternately sunny or shady.

CHAPTER 7

THE JOHNSON'S FERRY NORTH UNIT - FLOWERS IN THE SPRING

Directions to the Johnson's Ferry North Unit

1. Take I-285 east to Exit 24 (Riverside Drive).
2. Turn left onto Riverside Drive, and cross the bridge over I-285.
3. Travel about 2.2 miles north on Riverside Drive until you reach the stoplight at Johnson's Ferry Road, after a steep downhill curve.
4. Turn left onto Johnson's Ferry Road, and travel 0.25 miles, crossing the river. Immediately after the river is a stoplight at Columns Drive.
5. Turn right at the stoplight into the parking lot for the Johnson's Ferry North Unit, and follow the entrance road past the pavilion to the trailhead.
6. From I-285 west, take Exit 24, and turn right onto Riverside Drive.
7. Follow the same directions above.

Activities

- Picnicking
- Fishing
- Family walks
- Hiking
- Trail running
- Wildlife observation

- Boat launch
- Biking
- Running on nearby Columns Drive

Trails

- An loop walk through the floodplain area next to the river of about 1.8 miles with the chance to observe wildflowers in the spring (easy)

Unique Sights

- Creeks
- The river
- Wildlife
- Wildflowers

Facilities

- Pavilion
- Trails
- Trash cans
- Picnic tables
- Boat launch

Consisting of about one hundred acres, the Johnson's Ferry North Unit is a bit larger than the south unit and provides a longer hike for those seeking solitude. Numerous creeks flow down toward the river across this unit, providing nourishing water for many wildflowers in the springtime. In all, four small creeks feed into the river here: Nannyberry Creek, Arrowhead Creek, Owl Creek, and Mulberry Creek. The last one is the largest, providing a good flow of water into the Chattahoochee River at the far end of the unit.

The sole hike found in this unit is a wonderful place to identify wildflowers in the spring. There are also many flowers to be seen here in the fall. The observant hiker with a flower guide can identify many species along the moist trail. The hike itself is a loop providing views of the neighboring forest and river views too. There is little elevation change in the trail; therefore, it is an easy one for kids and those with less hiking experience. There is a utility cut through this area that does detract a bit from the beauty of the hike, but it is easily ignored by those seeking to observe nature. Bikes are not allowed on the trail in this unit; however, it is easy to access the Columns Drive road biking area from this unit by merely crossing Johnson's Ferry Road at the convenient crosswalk.

Like its southern neighbor, this unit is easily accessible and infrequently visited when compared with the Cochran Shoals Unit to the south.

Trail Option 1
Loop-Woods Hike
(1.80-Mile Loop—Easy)

I like to explore this area in the spring when wildflowers, such as catesby's trillium, toadshade trillium (spotted wake-robin), bluets, violets, and phlox, begin to appear trailside. In the fall, look for other flowering species such as spotted jewelweed and cardinal flower. This is a short hike that can be completed in an hour, but there is reason to linger here and explore. The beginning of the trail, in particular, is quite interesting. Those who enjoy flower photography, as I do, will want to bring a camera in the spring and, perhaps, in the fall too.

In the past, this trail has been known as the Mulberry Creek–loop trail, but there is little evidence of that name near the trailhead now. The trail is blue-blazed, but the blazes are infrequent and, sometimes, hard to see.

The trail starts off at the far end of the parking lot. Look for flowers of many sorts in the springtime where the trail begins. Even the parking lot itself and the fields around it can be resplendent with beautiful little blooms in March and April. Go around or through the metal gate appearing at 0.03 miles onto a wide trail that is large enough for vehicles and covered with gravel. You will note blackberry bushes and honeysuckle in many areas alongside the beginning of the trail. In the fall, look for blooming flowers here too.

At about 0.12 miles, the wide gravel road bends to the left slightly and then crosses the first creek, Nannyberry Creek, near an old trail sign.

Immediately thereafter, the trail splits into three more narrow trails. The trail straight ahead is a utility cut, which you should ignore. The other two options are the two sides of the lollipop-loop trail. This description follows the trail to the left clockwise along the loop. You will be returning from the other side.

Almost immediately (at 0.15 miles), you will reach a boardwalk with a bridge over a side creek. Look for spotted jewelweed in the fall in this area. The dense foliage along this short boardwalk is interesting and provides shade. On the bridge portion of the boardwalk, you will have a view into a swampy area where dead beaver-gnawed old trees stand as creepy sentinels over the watery ground. This is an excellent area to linger. You may see dark waters from creek runoff that pond into the wetland during the rainy season. Just imagine the wildlife that calls this place its home. Watch for owls and deer in the evening and hawks, turtles, frogs, and squirrels during the day.

At about 0.16 miles from the trailhead, the boardwalk will end near an old blue blaze, and if you look back to the left, you will see the remains of some old stables on the left. Going off trail into the creek area above the stables provides one with the opportunity to view wetland flowers in the spring. If you decide to explore the old stables, watch out for snakes. Following the trail as it bends to the right, away from the boardwalk, and begins to parallel the river also provides a good opportunity to see flowers. In general, you will notice that the wetland areas are to the right of the trail and the hillside, to the left of the trail. Many flowers can be seen on the wetland side of the trail. There are yucca plants along the trail here too, as well as bamboo.

At about 0.3 miles into the hike, the trail takes a sharp turn near a bridge over a small creek. You will note a dirt mound to the right. Bypass the side trail to the left, unless you have the desire to explore off trail. At 0.4 miles, you will see extensive marshland to the right of the trail, particularly during the wet season. At 0.5 miles, you will reach a marshy area, with a drainage creek to the right of the trail. Walk carefully through here during the wet season.

At 0.6 miles, a side trail goes off to the left. Keep to the right on the main trail. You will see a drop off to the left into a creek, which holds some small largemouth bass and an occasional frog. You will shortly reach a right turn with a sewer cap on the left along the creek. In another tenth of a mile, you will reach the utility cut through the forest, where it crosses the creek at a large pipe. The author has seen water snakes and anoles in this area. The trail then circles around a depressed area and heads toward the river. The trail shortly splits, with the left fork going toward the river and the creek, but stay to the right to continue on the trail, which begins to parallel the river as it flows on the left.

Near the trail split, you may be able to look out into the river at the mouth of this final creek (Mulberry Creek), where it flows into the Chattahoochee River. At low water, you may be able to see a dark *V* in the river pointing downstream. This is the remains of a fish trap that early settlers built to harvest fish from this area.

The remainder of the trail twists through the forest along the riverbank. Benches are placed strategically for those who wish to relax and enjoy the riverside environment. At 0.9 miles, the trail breaks out into another pipe cut and crosses a drainage ditch before returning to the woods. At 1.25 miles, the trail crosses a second drainage ditch in the pipe cut, and it crosses the pipe cut again at 1.4 miles. The trail through this area is well marked and easy to follow. It is a wonderful area for a riverside stroll or, perhaps, to walk the dog.

At 1.5 miles, you will reach the original trail split and the end of the lollipop loop. Turn left, and follow the wide gravel access road back to the parking lot and trailhead at 1.8 miles.

Sidebar 1
Toadshade Trillium

One type of flower that is common in the early spring along the trails in the CRNRA is the toadshade trillium, also known as spotted wake-robin or the very similar Chattahoochee wake-robin. The Johnson's Ferry South Unit is the perfect place to spot this close-to-the-ground flower during March and April. It usually grows in clusters in moist areas where creeks or drainages are close by. The plant's beautifully mottled green leaves are three in number, as suggested by its name. Its three-petal flower is usually a dark maroon, often growing thin and straight upward from the center of the three leaves. It is easy to see the stamens and anthers inside the flower.

Although most trilliums in the southeastern United States appear in the Appalachian Mountain chain, about five species can be found in the coastal plain and piedmont areas of the southeast. One of these is the toadshade trillium, which is actually rather common in the CRNRA during certain months of the year. Another more uncommon variety that I have spotted many times in the CRNRA is catesby's trillium, which grows in many of the same areas as the toadshade trillium. The catesby's trillium has curved pinkish petals on flowers that droop below the leaves. The petals bend backward in the catesby's variety, similar to a bog lily.

Look for these flowers in March and April along the trail in the Johnson's Ferry South Unit for a half mile or more after the boardwalk ends. They are also very prevalent in the Cochran Shoals and Sope Creek Units.

In the spring, sun loving flowers populate the first part of the Johnson's Ferry North trail.

The Johnson's Ferry North Unit has a typical trailhead into the trail system.

The first part of the trail in the Johnson's Ferry North Unit is a wide gravel surface.

This old tree currently stands over the swampy wildlife area at the start of the Johnson's Ferry North hike.

This trail sign in the Johnson's Ferry North Unit is typical of CRNRA trail signs.

Orange jewelweed can be found on the forest's edge in the Johnson's Ferry North Unit.

The second half of the Johnson's Ferry North hike is characterized by sylvan river views.

CHAPTER 8

THE GOLD BRANCH UNIT - BULL SLUICE LAKE

Directions to the Gold Branch Unit

1. Take I-285 east or west to the Riverside Drive exit (Exit 24).
2. Go north on Riverside Drive (outside I-285) for about 2.5 miles to a four-way intersection with Johnson's Ferry Road at a traffic light just after a sharp bend in the road.
3. Turn left (north) on Johnson's Ferry Road, immediately crossing the river.
4. Travel 1.6 miles north on Johnson's Ferry Road to its intersection with Lower Roswell Road at a traffic light.
5. Turn right on Lower Roswell Road, and follow the road 3.2 miles to the entrance to the Gold Branch Unit on the right.

Activities

- Picnicking
- Fishing
- Family walks
- Hiking
- Trail running
- Wildlife observation

Trails

- A lollipop-loop walk of about 1.35 miles along the shores of Bull Sluice Lake with fine lake views and an optional, difficult visit to a huge rock shelter (moderate to difficult)
- A very nice hike through wooded terrain and along the lakeshore of about three miles (moderate)

Unique Sights

- Bull Sluice Lake
- Morgan Falls Dam
- Small creeks and waterslides
- Wildlife
- Large rock shelter
- Wildflowers

Facilities

- Picnic tables
- Activity field
- Trails

The Gold Branch Unit affords hikers and fishermen a network of trails that is both beautiful and accessible. Because hiking, trail running, fishing, and perhaps, paddling are the only real activities that are available in the Gold Branch Unit, it is less frequented than some of the other units, which affords the hiker the possibility of solitude and the fisherman the access to many fishing spots. The Gold Branch Unit has something of a Jekyll-and-Hyde network of trails. The interior trails through the young forest are some of the most gentle and relaxing trails in the CRNRA. However, the trails leading along the edge of Bull Sluice Lake are often difficult, uneven, and poorly marked. Nonetheless, hikes within this unit can be tailored to all tastes, and the trails are beautiful enough to be worth the extra effort that is sometimes required to hike them.

The main feature of the Gold Branch Unit is Bull Sluice Lake. The lake was impounded from the waters of the Chattahoochee River when

Morgan Falls Dam was constructed in 1904 by the Atlanta Water and Electric Power Company. The dam is 56 feet high and 1,075 feet long. It can be seen (on the lakeside) from the middle portion of the second hike described in this chapter. The trails in the Gold Branch Unit are all within a 358-acre spit of land that protrudes into Bull Sluice Lake. Therefore, no matter which trail you take, if you keep hiking, you will end up at Bull Sluice Lake or back at the trailhead.

Wet-weather creeks cascade down off the rolling hills of this land into sheltered coves in Bull Sluice Lake. Some of the seven miles of trails in the Gold Branch Unit parallel these creeks. Others ramble through the woods above the lake. The longest stretch of trail extends virtually all the way around the unit's lakeshore within the boundaries of the unit, and this circumnavigation is a possibility for those who are fit and adventurous. As mentioned above, the lakeshore portions of the trail are often difficult and, in some places, amount to nothing more than used trails. But the lakeshore trails are definitely worth taking and should be fully explored by those with the physical capacity to hike them. There are also marshy areas in this unit, an example of which can be seen near the trailhead.

Wildlife is plentiful in Gold Branch, as in other units of the CRNRA. However, in this unit, there are even more opportunities to see animals because the wildlife population is supported by a larger-than-normal number of fruit- and nut-bearing trees. Birds, including songbirds, woodpeckers, hawks, owls, ducks, geese, and herons, frequent these environs. Deer are not uncommon. Smaller animals, such as beavers, rabbits, opossums, squirrels, and raccoon, are also present, although some (particularly raccoon and opossums) are usually nocturnal. One also has the opportunity to see various reptiles and amphibians during the spring and summer seasons in this unit. Be sure to check for wildflowers in the spring, particularly around the many wet areas leading to the lake.

The trails in the Gold Branch Unit are interconnecting, so various hikes can be tailored based upon the amount of time that a hiker has to visit the area and other factors. Bikes are not allowed on the trails in the Gold Branch Unit, but trail running and dog walking are permitted. Unlike some of the other units, such as Sope Creek, Cochran Shoals, Powers Island, Palisades East, and Palisades West, there are no major historic structural ruins near the trails in this unit. The pleasure here comes mostly from nature.

Whether you come for a relaxing stroll, a trail run, a fishing experience, or a challenging hike, the Gold Branch Unit has opportunities that you will enjoy.

Trail Option 1
Short but Potentially Difficult Lollipop Loop along Lakeshore (1.7 Miles—Moderate to Difficult, Depending upon whether One Visits the Rock Shelter)

This trail has a fairly easy lead-in of 0.5 miles, followed by 0.2 miles of very rough, used trail if you decide to visit a massive rock outcrop that may have been used by indigenous peoples for shelter. The final 0.6 miles of this trail travel along easy lakeshore trail then uphill along a moderate grade on an established trail and back down to the trailhead. The main attractions of this loop are many views of Bull Sluice Lake and its coves, as well as the rock shelter, which is very interesting to explore. This hike also provides shaded woods that are pleasant for hiking and wildlife observation. For those who are unable to hike the rough section of this loop, there is a detour around the roughest section near the rock shelter, and there are other routes that will take you in shorter loops back to the trailhead or onto easier trails. You can fashion your own hike, but I found this one interesting enough to highlight.

The hike begins at the lone established trailhead at the far end of the unit's parking lot. There are the usual trailhead signs and notices here, which provide information concerning your hike. This trailhead leads quickly into the entire Gold Branch trail system. The trailhead is located in a power cut, which provides a field that can be used for activities. There are also a couple of picnic tables for quick meals in the spring and fall when the weather is generally nicer.

Enter the woods near the signs, and immediately go downhill on a couple of switchbacks with stairs zigzagging down into a small drainage creek area. The wide and well-used trail parallels the creek, which will be on your left, until you reach a boardwalk over the creek at about 0.09 miles. The boardwalk crosses both the creek and the wetland area around the creek. This can be a good area to look for wetland plants and animals, and the creek itself flows into Bull Sluice Lake. Just after the boardwalk ends, you will reach a signed trail junction, which you should follow to your left downhill and along the creek. The trail is blue-blazed, initially wide and flat and will initially parallel the wet and muddy creek drainage.

At 0.16 miles, one passes the first curiosity along the trail. Someone has faintly painted the word "terror" on a rock to the right of the trail as you begin a short staircase up onto a shoulder of a hill. Why anyone would consider this hike to inspire terror, I am not sure. However, at 0.18 miles, the hiker will pass over a nice wood bridge over a dry drainage (which appears troll-free), and at 0.24 miles, a muddy clearing can be observed down to the left near the creek drainage. At about the same point, you will gain your first view of Bull Sluice Lake, although this area of the lake is nothing more than a back cove. You will see a lot more of the lake before this hike is finished.

At 0.26 miles, you will cross another wooden bridge near the lakeshore and then reach an unsigned trail intersection with a primitive trail along the lakeshore. Go to the right and uphill a short way, following the blue blazes and admiring the forest canopy. There will be some short wooden stairs in this area too. At 0.28 miles, you will reach a signed trail intersection, at which you should go to the left and begin paralleling the lakeshore more closely. This section consists of rolling hills, and fishermen will find numerous places to sneak down to the lake to try their luck. At 0.30 miles, you will pass a blue blaze on your left and go uphill for a short way to a rockier area. At 0.38 miles, you will still be paralleling the lakeshore until you reach a signed intersection at 0.44 miles at a nice flat point along the lakeshore. Go left at this intersection as a right turn will lead you away from the lake and back into the woods.

Continue to follow the trail around the lakeshore. You will shortly reach another nice spot with a view of the lake and an opening for fishing. Then, at about 0.48 miles from the trailhead, the trail becomes rougher and rockier. The trail splits at about this point, with a used trail scaling the hillside above the lakeshore, and the blue-blazed main trail goes to the right uphill, skirting the hillside higher above. It is at this point that you have a choice. If you want to stay on the maintained trail and miss the rock shelter, keep to your right, and follow the main blue-blazed trail through the woods. If you are up for a short adventure, follow the used trail along the hillside closer to the water.

If you choose the used trail, it will descend and then ascend into some mountain laurel. At 0.54 miles from the trailhead, the used trail will have ascended almost to the level of the main trail. Continue to scale the hillside on the used trail, and you will almost immediately come to the rock forming the top of the rock shelter. It is a somewhat treacherous descent from here on a muddy slope to the bottom of the overhang, but it is worth the effort. The massive rock shelter is large enough to have given shelter to native peoples many years ago. Imagine how life for these people must have been affected by the weather conditions and by the movement of animals and the existence of nearby water. This shelter is one of the largest along the Chattahoochee River, although there are such numerous shelters as detailed elsewhere in this book.

When you are ready to go back to the main trail, ascend the hillside right next to the far side of the overhanging rock of the shelter. You will first reach a used trail, which you should avoid and cross over, and keep ascending straight up through the brush on the hillside until you reach the blue-blazed main trail. You will then be about 0.59 miles from the trailhead. Like the descent into the rock shelter, this ascent is also somewhat treacherous and should only be attempted by those who are nimble enough to do some climbing and bushwhacking. Once you reach the main trail, turn to the left, and once again, parallel the lakeshore (although you will be far above the lake initially). You will be glad that the hiking has changed back to easy-to-moderate walking for a while.

The trail travels slowly downhill until it begins to parallel the lakeshore again at 0.61 miles. The trail travels through some nice upland woods with a downhill that is not steep. The lake will be ever-present on your left, and you may be able to see various waterbirds in the shallow areas or, perhaps, on the island just off the shore. You may be lucky enough to see kayakers in the water in this area or, perhaps, a fisherman. At 0.69 miles, the nonblazed, used trail will come in from the left—keep to the right along the lakeshore.

At 0.73 miles, you will cross a dry drainage; shortly afterward, look for a clearly beaver-chewed tree on the left down near the lakeshore. Obviously, beavers are hard at work in this area of the lake. At 0.80 miles, there is a nice lake view of the cove and island found in this part of the lake. This is a good place to observe Canadian geese. Turn to the right at the lakeshore at 0.87 miles where there are some more nice views, and at 0.89 miles, you will reach a signed intersection with a blue-blazed trail leading to the right uphill into the woods away from the lake. Savor your last views of the lake here. The trail straight ahead leads along the lakeshore and can be taken on a much longer hike to circumnavigate the Gold Branch Unit near the lakeshore. However, for this hike, turn to the right, and go uphill into the forest.

After a moderate climb, the trail will flatten out on a ridge at about 1.03 miles. Enjoy the splendid woods and isolation in this area. At 1.06 miles, you will reach a signed T intersection with a central trail. Go to the left through a sylvan area on flat trail. After you enjoy this short section, you will reach another signed intersection at 1.11 miles. Turn to the right here onto a blue-blazed, graded trail through more nice forests along a hillside, which turns downhill with stairs. At 1.25 miles, you will reach a signed intersection that completes the loop and leads toward the trailhead. You can see the boardwalk near the trailhead on your left. Turn left here onto the boardwalk, and ascend back up to the trailhead and parking lot at 1.35 miles. Savor this short walk as a great break from the hustle and bustle of the city of Atlanta. It can be combined with other trails in the area to make for a longer hike too.

Trail Option 2
Wooded Lakeshore–Loop Trail
(3.0 Miles—Moderate)

This hike of nearly three miles showcases much of the best of the Gold Branch Unit. The first mile or so traverses nice piedmont forest, including some areas that clearly have been hit by heavy winds. The next 1.2 miles consist of a beautiful lakeshore trail that can be very rough at times but rewarding with nice views of the lake. The remainder of the hike follows creek drainage back into the forest away from the lake and then descends to the trailhead through nice forest. This is a hike for those who want to get away from it all for an afternoon. I rarely see more than a couple of people on this hike. Enjoy.

The hike begins at the main trailhead at the far end of the Gold Branch parking lot. Hike downhill along the switchbacks to the boardwalk described above over the creek drainage at 0.09 miles. Cross the boardwalk, and reach a signed intersection on the far side, where you will turn right and go uphill on a sustained moderate grade with some steps through nice forest. You will reach a second signed intersection at about 0.3 miles in a nice forested section. Turn right here on a level and gentle blue-blazed trail through the woods. Enjoy the forest walk here as it is easier hiking than that up ahead.

At 0.36 miles, begin a short downhill section, and arrive at a signed intersection on the left for a trail that travels downhill into a creek drainage at 0.4 miles. This is the trail on which you will be returning to complete the loop. Proceed straight ahead. You may note some houses on the right through the woods as the trail is, at this point, nearly at the boundary of the NRA unit. The trail rolls along the ridgeline of an old roadbed until it reaches yet another signed intersection at 0.57 miles, where you should go to the right for the complete loop. (A shorter loop can be accomplished by taking a left turn here and hiking to the lakeshore and then returning up the return trail noted above.)

As you walk along the old roadbed of the trail, you can wonder who it was that initially graded this trail. Was it an early settler in this area or perhaps someone who wanted access to the river before the impounding of Bull Sluice Lake? You will note more houses off to the right at about 0.74 miles, particularly in the wintertime. The long gentle trail continues to be suitable for family walks all the way to the 0.83-mile mark. Make sure to bend sharply to the left at a confusing intersection marked by shot-up metal scraps on the right. A right turn here may lead to the housing area.

At 0.83 miles, the trail begins to descend to the river, mildly at first. After the initial descent, the trail passes through an area that was recently, heavily damaged by wind at 0.88 miles. In this area, many downed trees have been cleared off the trail, opening up a larger view of the area than usually afforded by the forest. Was it a downdraft that pushed over these trees or an actual tornado? At 0.94 miles, the trail actually goes through almost a tunnel of downed trees. As the years progress, this tunnel of trees will give way to gravity, but for now, it makes for an interesting hiker tunnel. Begin another gentle downhill at 1.0 miles, and reach a winter view of Bull Sluice Lake shortly thereafter. The trail then begins a much steeper downhill and bends to the left. You will be able to see the lakeside of the Morgan Falls Dam at this point and during the next segment of this hike.

Morgan Falls Dam is an impressive structure, even from the lakeside. It was constructed in 1904 by the Atlanta Water and Electric Power Company. It stands 56 feet high and is 1,075 feet long. For a better view of the dam from its riverside, take Morgan Falls Road, which can be reached from Roswell Road, just north of Sandy Springs. There is good trout fishing in the tailwaters in this area.

After the final, very steep downhill section, the trail reaches lake level at 1.17 miles. At this point, the trail becomes a jaunt along the lakeshore and the various scenic coves created by water draining downslope into the lake. As the trail meanders in a parallel path with the lakeshore, it also becomes more difficult to negotiate and rocky. This portion of the trail is difficult for those with limited physical capacity, and hikers should plan accordingly. However, the beauty of the intersection between forest and lake is worth the extra effort.

Shortly after the trail reaches the lakeshore, look for a huge and impressive pine tree to the right of the trail. How long has this tree stood guard in the forest? Without scientific testing, one can only wonder. At 1.22 miles, the trail reaches a small cove with a trickle of water flowing into the lake. At this point, the main river channel becomes more obvious when looking out into the lake. The next section of lakeshore trail is characterized by rock outcrops and by yucca plants alongside the trail. At 1.55 miles, watch the lakeshore for tree stumps that have clearly been chewed by beavers.

At 1.69 miles, you will reach a sweet surprise gift from the trail. You will cross logs over a beautiful cascade at the head of a sheltered cove on the lake. Take time to savor this location. This is precisely why I love to hike. Often, trails will reveal secret delights to those who venture far from the trailhead. Sometimes, as with this hike, the delightful find is subtle and secretive. This spot will probably be yours alone for as long as you choose to linger. Enjoy it as long as you can before heading farther along the trail.

At 1.75 miles, the trail reaches a signed intersection with a trail heading off to the left, away from the lake. If you take this trail, it will bring you back to the trail you came in on, where you should turn right if you wish to return to your car. However, to continue this hike, continue straight ahead along the lakeshore, following the blue blazes. At 1.98 miles, the trail passes another large pine tree on the right, and at 2.06 miles, it reaches the head of another small and sheltered cove. It follows the small cove stream upstream, where there are more cascades in the sylvan stream. At 2.18 miles, the trail reaches a wood bridge at the head of a third cove, where it crosses yet another wet-weather stream flowing down toward the lake.

At 2.20 miles, the trail reaches another signed T intersection with a trail heading to the left. Proceed to the left and uphill on an obvious old roadbed. You will be leaving Bull Sluice Lake behind at this point and traveling deeper into the forest. The trail generally parallels a small wet-weather stream on a gentle uphill in a nice forest. At 2.45 miles, the trail reaches a signed intersection with the trail leading into this hike. Go to the right here to return to the trailhead and parking lot. At 2.54 miles, turn left at another signed intersection, and proceed on a steady downhill to the final, signed intersection at 2.71 miles near the boardwalk. Turn left here at the final intersection; cross the boardwalk, and reach the trailhead at 2.82 miles. This hike is long enough to make you feel pleasantly tired afterward.

Young hikers prepare at the trailhead to explore the Gold Branch Unit.

The trailhead at the Gold Branch Unit features typical signs.

An early bridge greets hikers in the Gold Branch Unit.

Young hikers can climb the trailside rocks in the Gold Branch Unit.

Some trails run alongside Bull Sluice Lake in the Gold Branch Unit.

Typical wintertime trail in the Gold Branch Unit.

Some of the lakeside trails in the Gold Branch Unit are remote and peaceful.

This tree tunnel can be found among the downed trees in one section of the Gold Branch Unit.

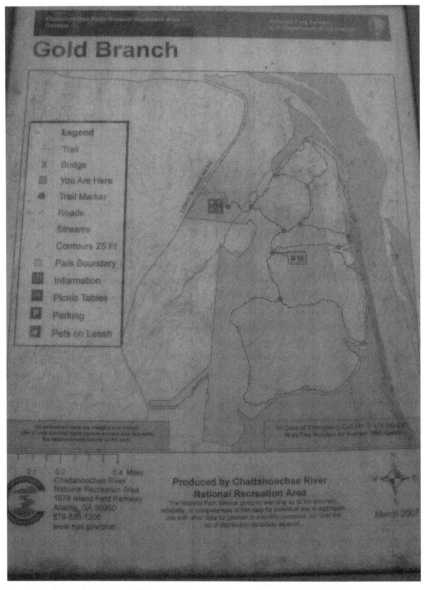

A typical trail intersection sign keeps hikers on track in the Gold Branch Unit.

Interesting ground cover in the Gold Branch Unit.

This trailhead sign shows hikers what to expect in the Gold Branch Unit.

CHAPTER 9

THE VICKERY CREEK UNIT - HISTORY AND ROSWELL AREA TRAILS

Directions to the Vickery Creek Unit

1. Take I-285 east or west to GA 400 north to Exit 6—Northridge Road.
2. Go around the looping ramp, staying to the far right, merging onto Northridge Road, going west.
3. Continue for less than a mile on Northridge Road, ignoring the signs for the CRNRA, until you reach a dead end on Roswell Road (GA Highway 9).
4. Turn right, and go north on Roswell Road about two miles until you cross the river.
5. To reach the southern entrance into the unit and its trailhead, turn right onto Riverside Road immediately after crossing the river, and go for a short distance, where you will find the entrance on your left, down a short gravel drive.
6. To reach the mill ruins entrance and trailhead, you should proceed about one mile on Roswell Road after crossing the river.
7. Turn right onto Mill Street, and proceed downhill a short way to an intersection, where you will turn right again and follow the road downhill to the paved parking area and trailhead near some buildings.

8. To reach the Oxbo Road entrance into the unit and its trailhead, follow the directions for the Mill Street entrance, but proceed for another 0.5 miles north on Roswell Road past Mill Street.
9. When you reach Oxbo Road on your right, turn right onto it, and drive for 0.5 miles to a parking area on the right, or for a better parking area, drive 1.0 miles from the Roswell Road turnoff, to Dobbs Drive on the left.
10. Turn left onto Dobbs Drive, and proceed uphill into Waller Park.
11. About 0.3 miles after the turn onto Dobbs Drive, you will turn right onto Dobbs Court, at the sign for the soccer practice area.
12. Follow Dobbs Court straight ahead, and look for the Oxbo trailhead under a trellis at the end of the parking area.

Activities

- Picnicking
- Fishing
- Family walks
- Hiking
- Trail running
- Wildlife observation
- Exploring Mill ruins

Trails

- A lead-in trail of about half a mile at the southern entrance leads to the full trail system (easy to moderate)
- A lollipop-loop walk of about 1.5 miles from the mill ruins entrance with excellent forest and wildlife-viewing opportunities and the chance to explore the mill ruins (easy to moderate)

A longer lollipop stroll of nearly two miles starting at the Oxbo Road/Waller Park entrance showcasing some of the best forest paths in the unit (moderate)

Unique Sights

- Roswell Mill ruins and dam
- Ivy Woolen Mill ruins
- Allenbrook
- Vickery Creek
- Wildlife
- Excellent forest
- Some wildflowers

Facilities

- Picnic tables
- Restrooms
- Roswell Mill ruins
- Bridges over Vickery Creek
- Nearby restaurants
- Trails

The Vickery Creek Unit is a spectacular venue for hiking, particularly for those who enjoy history and those who enjoy a nice posthike meal and drinks. The unit consists of about 254 acres—enough to shelter white-tailed deer, foxes, owls, hawks, and other large animals. Although the unit is surrounded by the civilization of the city of Roswell and its environs, it is still quite possible to gain solitude here on some of the less traveled trails, particularly during the week. Because the unit is surrounded by roads, it is difficult to get too lost here. In addition, visitors to this unit can explore the history of the Roswell Manufacturing Company's dam and ruins, the site of the Ivy Woolen Mill, and Allenbrook (which dates back to about 1840). Two nice bridges also span Vickery Creek, where hikers can gain pretty views of the creek area and rapids. Sun worshippers also enjoy the rocks in the creek on warm summer days. The Vickery Creek Unit has something for everyone.

The hikes found in the Vickery Creek Unit are usually not very strenuous. Generally, the trails consist of pleasant meandering forest walks. However, there are short steep stretches in some areas. Vickery Creek is a nice place to go after work for a hike of one to three miles. Most of the trails hide within the tree canopy, so overheating is generally not a problem.

On summer evenings, while walking in Vickery Creek, I have heard barred owls bring the forest to life with their hooting, and I have seen an owl or two while hiking there. Go as late in the evening as you can in order to see wildlife. On one evening hike, I saw three deer and a barred owl at the same time.

The historical elements of this unit are treasures to explore with the whole family. See the sidebar below for more information. The ruins of the Roswell Manufacturing Company's mill can be easily explored as they surround the Mill Street entrance to the unit. The dam, original machine shop, and some mill equipment can be viewed along the interpretive trail near the parking area, which is on the other side of the covered bridge from the main trail system. The ruins of the Ivy Woolen Mill can be discovered (although not much remains) near the confluence of Vickery Creek and the Chattahoochee River, along the riverside near the intersection of Roswell Road and Riverside Drive. Allenbrook, a small brick house along Roswell Road, housed the manager of the Ivy Woolen Mill. It can be accessed by a separate entrance off S. Atlanta Street (Roswell Road). It has some short trails leading off the back into the woods near the creek.

Another unique feature of this unit is that parking for hiking at the Mill Street and Waller Park entrances is free of charge, which makes this unit more attractive to those who do not want to buy a yearly park pass and who don't happen to have the usual parking money in their vehicle or pocket.

I would recommend the trails in this unit for trail running or for hikes in the fall or spring. In the summer, this unit is perfect for an after-work evening hike, listening for hawks and owls, and watching for deer and other animals. There are some wildflowers in this unit; however, do not expect the showy displays of wildflowers that can be found in some other units. The forest canopy here restricts the number of wildflowers. Although the trail system does not permit bicycles, it is rather popular with weekend walkers in the warmer months. For more solitude, hike on weekdays or forge deeper into the trail system. You will be glad you did so.

Trail Option 1
Riverside Drive–Entrance Trail
(0.5 Miles Each Way—Easy to Moderate)

The entrance to the unit off Riverside Drive provides a short gravel drive into a parking area. From this parking area, the network of trails in the Vickery Creek Unit can be accessed. You may want to start a day hike from this area in order to see the area from a new vantage point or in order to avoid the more crowded Mill Street entrance.

The lead-in hike starts at the far end of the parking area and passes the usual trailhead signs. Initially, the trail is flat, and it parallels the downstream end of the creek. Because of the proximity to the river, the creek through this area is slow-moving. Watch for wildlife, despite the proximity of several busy roads. You may see tulips blooming in this area in February and March.

In about 0.03 miles, the trail reaches a signed intersection. For the main trail, you will turn right and go up the inground stairs. If you were to follow the trail straight ahead or to the right (as my kids and I did one February afternoon), you would find that the trail parallels the creek for about 0.25 miles through heavy undergrowth. It ends at a cliff area where this used trail cannot access. The end of the accessible used trail is signaled by a sign and a cable. Despite the short distance, this used trail may provide interesting exploration for plants and flowers in the spring.

Back at the signed intersection, the trail switchbacks uphill to the right. At 0.08 miles, it switchbacks sharply to the left to the top of the hill and then begins to skirt along the hill. At 0.16 miles, the trail reaches a flat old roadbed and a bench or two. This is a nice place to relax and stay a while, away from the hustle and bustle of city life. The trail becomes a nice flat walk along the hillside with the creek far below. There are some nice winter views here across the creek to the opposite hillside below Allenbrook.

At 0.35 miles, the trail reaches a second nice bench on the right-hand side and some more good winter views. The trail then bends to the right, away from the creek, and begins to parallel a dry creek drainage on the left. This is an area of nice young growth forest. The trail begins a slight uphill, until at about 0.5 miles, it reaches a signed T intersection with other trails in the unit's trail system. From here, you can branch out into the rest of the area's trails for a hike as long or as short as you wish. If you have come for a short stroll, return for 0.5 miles back to your car the way you came.

Trail Option 2
Lollipop-Loop Walk from Mill Street Entrance
(1.5 Miles—Easy to Moderate)

This is a really nice trail that has very few moderate sections and no strenuous sections that lead through the heart of the Vickery Creek Unit. I have enjoyed this hike many times, and I especially like it because, like some of the other hikes in this book, it brings the hiker into a truly natural-feeling area without much effort. Midway through this hike, you will feel much farther out into the woods than you actually are. To me, this is the hallmark of a classic CRNRA hike, and busy Atlanta residents should really embrace this type of hike. The trees and wildlife found on this hike are a bonus as are the shorter distance and easy nature of the trail.

To start this hike, park in the free Mill Street parking lot (if you can find a parking space), and go downhill to the wooden trellis that marks the beginning of the trail system access. Begin your hike by going through the trellis and downhill on a paved path past a nice overlook of the creek and the surrounding area. At 0.03 miles, you can turn left (actually straight ahead) to follow the path to the milldam and raceway on a gravel path with interpretive signs, where you can also view some of the mill machinery. At the intersection at 0.03 miles, you can see the former machine shop building right in front of you. To continue the hike, turn right, and go downhill on the paved path to the covered bridge over Vickery Creek. Cross the bridge while savoring the view of this area. This is truly one of the most scenic places in any of the CRNRA units.

On the far side of the bridge, you will find a trail sign and some concrete stairs. Take those uphill, and follow the dirt trail up as it curves to the left. At about 0.05 miles, you will pass a signed trail coming in from the left, which runs along the hillside parallel with the creek. Do not take this trail to the left, but proceed straight ahead and uphill. Shortly thereafter, you will reach a Y intersection. If you proceed to the right, the trail will be a flat, graded, and blue-blazed trail that eventually leads downhill to another intersection. Rather than going right at the Y, take the left fork instead. You will bear uphill on a washed-out dirt trail with roots. The trail flattens out at about 0.11 miles, and this is where one can begin to really enjoy the forest setting of this hike. Many oak trees make their home here.

At 0.29 miles, there will be a bench on the right-hand side of the trail, followed quickly by a signed intersection with a trail to the left. Proceed straight ahead, continuing to enjoy the forest setting and quiet solitude. This part of the trail is flat and enjoyable for all hikers. It bends to the left, passes a wooden fence on the right-hand side, and at 0.39 miles, reaches another signed intersection with a trail coming in from the left. Again, go straight or to the right to continue the hike. At 0.45 miles, the trail reaches yet another signed intersection with a trail coming in from the left, where one should continue straight or to the right. The trail coming in from the left-hand side here is the return trail that finishes the lollipop loop.

Continue on the nice, level trail through beautiful woods. Check out the muscadine vines that are prevalent here and all along this trail. At 0.53 miles, the trail reaches another signed intersection, this time with a trail coming in from the right-hand side. The trail heading to the right is flat and appears to be blazed. Go instead to the left or straight ahead, passing another used trail to the right, which appears to approach the CRNRA boundary, and a CRNRA trail sign with Vickery Creek Unit regulations.

Shortly after the sign, the trail will go downhill and then begin to skirt some hills through the forest while crossing through shallow valleys and dry drainages. There will be at least one very brief, steep uphill on dirt trail, followed by a brief, steep downhill. You will notice a house and a road to your right, if you are observant and/or if it is winter. This area is another fine forested walk. By 0.7 miles, you will reach a signed intersection with a CRNRA Regulations sign. A turn to the right appears to lead out of the CRNRA. Go left here. You will get another brief glimpse of the road at about 0.78 miles.

At 0.82 miles, the trail reaches another signed intersection. The main trail leads to the right (straight ahead), whereas a narrower smaller trail leads uphill. Take the left turn onto a gradual uphill back toward the deep forest. After some level and pretty forest, walking on narrow trail, there will be some more open areas that appear to hold wild raspberries in the fall and muscadine vines. At 0.95 miles, there is an old corral to the left of the trail that merits further exploration. Could this area be the remains of an old homestead or homesite? Continue to follow the trail along the crest of a low small ridgeline through immature forest. There will be a very short easy uphill and then some downhill at about 1.08 miles. By 1.11 miles, the trail reaches the end of the lollipop loop at the intersection noted above. Hopefully, you have enjoyed being in nature without much exertion needed to enjoy the remote-feeling surroundings.

Turn to the right at the intersection, and retrace your steps back to the covered bridge, which you will reach at 1.46 miles. At 1.53 miles, the parking lot is reached. Make sure to take time to explore the history around Mill Street before leaving. Once you have done so, you can feel satisfied that you have seen the best of both history and nature in the area.

Trail Option 3
Longer Lollipop-Loop Stroll from Oxbo/Waller Park Entrance
(1.9 Miles—Moderate)

This hike showcases some of the best and remotest hiking in the Vickery Creek Unit, without requiring too much commitment than the previous hike. It should be savored, although the beginning of the hike requires a walk along sometimes-busy Oxbo Road. I have seen a lot of wildlife on this hike, and if you are quiet and hike in the early morning or evening, you may too. This hike also has the advantage of starting at a parking area that is free.

The hike starts from the Oxbo Road/Waller Park entrance. Park your car in the spaces at the end of the side road in Waller Park near the practice soccer fields. I have played many soccer games at Waller Park, and the practice fields are used by many teams to keep in shape for regular-season games. At the end of the side road parking lot, you will see a wooden trellis with the words "Oxbo Trail" prominently displayed on its top. Walk through this trellis to start your hike. The trail on this side of Oxbo Road is clearly on an old roadbed that descends rapidly on gravel and dirt from Waller Park to the level of Oxbo Road. There are some interesting rocks in the old road cut to the left of the trail as it descends.

At 0.12 miles, the trail reaches Oxbo Road. Cross the road here to access the sidewalk on the opposite side of the road, and turn right on the sidewalk. As you walk on the sidewalk, you will be between Vickery Creek and Oxbo Road, paralleling both. There has been some sidewalk-repair work here in the recent past, so be careful, especially with oncoming traffic. At 0.27 miles, the sidewalk passes a dam on the creek and an apparent power station. Shortly thereafter, you should turn left onto a nice metal-and-wood pedestrian bridge spanning the creek. There is a good view of the dam from the bridge. Linger here if you like.

At the far side of the bridge, there is a trailside kiosk as the now dirt trail immediately turns uphill into the forest, navigating tree roots and wood stairs. At 0.33 miles from Waller Park, there is a signed T intersection in the trail. Turn to the right here onto a wide trail that provides easy hiking. Begin to observe the forest environment as the trail moves deeper into the cool shade of the woods. At 0.44 miles, the trail reaches a four-way intersection. The intersection is marked by an interesting tree on the left-hand side that has sprouted four separate trees. A turn to the right here takes one on a gradual downhill that becomes steeper and rockier toward the end. You can see the road and the creek from the narrow trails in this area that provide ample opportunity for exploration (and possibly wild raspberries), should you be so inclined. However, to continue this hike, turn to the left at the four-way intersection with the odd four-way tree.

Upon turning left, you will begin hiking on a smooth wide trail that runs along a shallow ridgetop through an oak forest with occasional patches of pine seedlings in some clearings. This is a very pleasant and easy stroll. By the 0.56-mile mark, you may note a profusion of large dead pine trees that are providing nutrients to the soil of the forest, where younger trees have begun to predominate. Watch for wildlife as you traverse this area. Recently, I walked up on two young deer and a barred owl along this area of the trail. The owl gave me a good opportunity to watch it as he sat on a branch above the trail, scanning the area.

At 0.65 miles, the trail begins a mild downhill, and at 0.80 miles, bear left at an unsigned intersection with a used trail, following the blue-blazed loop through more nice forests. At 0.91 miles, the trail reaches a T intersection. The trail to the right goes down and deeper into the trail system. Turn to the left instead here to continue to follow the loop trail. The trail will go up slightly, curve to the right, and then go down mildly but steadily. At 0.98 miles, you will note a blue blaze on the right, and you will soon discover that you are nearing a road. There may be some wet areas in the trail here if the Georgia rains have persisted. You will also continue to see downed trees alongside the trail. These downed trees provide fertile areas for insects, animals, and plants to survive.

At 1.10 miles, the trail reaches a signed T intersection near CRNRA information signs and boards. A turn to the right here goes about forty yards to Grimes Bridge Road. Bear left instead, and go downhill at first.

The trail reaches another signed intersection at 1.13 miles with a trail on the right that leads downward to the edge of the creek. To enjoy creek exploration, turn right here. To otherwise follow the intended loop, proceed straight ahead rather than turning right. In this area, the trail begins a series of moderate ups and downs. The hilltops occur at regular intervals, as do the valleys. The valleys are generally filled with wet-weather stream bottoms, which are great places to find salamanders. The hilltops can be great places to listen for animals. The buzz of cicadas is ever-present here in the summertime. On one hike in this area, I listened for minutes as numerous barred owls spoke with each other in their typical "hoo, hoo, hoo-hooooo" calls. It was fascinating to listen to the slight differences between the calls of individual owls.

Some of the slopes in this area of the hike can be a bit rocky, but each of the upslope and downslope is not too long. By the 1.4-mile mark, the trail finally begins to flatten out and, after one more rocky dip and climb, reaches a signed T intersection. Turn to the right here, and go down the trail back to the pedestrian bridge over Vickery Creek at 1.55 miles. On the other side of the bridge, turn right on the sidewalk, and parallel the road, noting the picnic tables, benches, decks, and trails along the creek. At 1.76 miles, cross Oxbo Road, and go up the old roadbed trail back to your car at Waller Park.

This trail refreshes one's appetite for the outdoors without too much commitment. In very few areas around Atlanta can you have this much nature for so little effort.

Sidebar 1
Roswell History

As stated previously, the Vickery Creek Unit contains valuable history lessons on the city of Roswell and the Civil War. The easiest historical area to explore is the ruins of the Roswell Manufacturing Company's mill on Vickery Creek near the Mill Street entrance to the unit. The area to explore is along the creek downhill from the parking area. The old building standing next to the covered bridge is the original machine shop, the only building to survive. Along the creek bank to the right (when facing the covered bridge) are more ruins. But the main area of exploration is upstream from the covered bridge along the interpretive trail. Here you will find mill machinery and walls, along with the dam. The waterfall over the dam can make a beautiful photograph in the spring or fall. Take time to explore and read the interpretive signs.

According to the interpretive signs, in 1835, Roswell King came to this area of former Cherokee Nation Land with his son, Barrington King. They anticipated starting a planned community called the Colony. In 1839, they incorporated the Roswell Manufacturing Company, one of the earliest textile mills in what was then Cobb County (although the area is now in Fulton County). In 1839, the mill had 30 workers, but it had swollen to 250 workers by 1853, and 400 by the Civil War. The mill produces mainly shirting, sheeting, yarn, and coarse, heavy cloth.

Constructed in 1839 and 1853, the Roswell Manufacturing Company mill buildings were burned by civil war Union forces on July 7, 1864. The 1853 mill was rebuilt after the war but was destroyed by fire in 1926. The mill helped the early town of Roswell earn a name as one of the most important manufacturing towns in Georgia. It is likely this reputation that led Union troops to the area during the Civil War. The mill utilized its dam on Vickery Creek to provide power for its operations. Today, the dam provides a scenic backdrop for folks relaxing along the creek. Please stay behind barriers to prevent injury. The dam is easily visible from areas around the creek near the Mill Street entrance. A wonderful view can be found from the covered bridge spanning the creek here, which leads into the unit's trail system.

Another bit of history near this unit is the ruins of the Ivy Woolen Mill. The ruins can be located along the banks of the Chattahoochee River near the confluence of Vickery Creek and the river and near the intersection of Roswell Road and Riverside Drive. Take care when exploring here, as this area is overgrown except for a nice recently constructed boardwalk trail leading to a dock on the river bank.

At the time of the Civil War, the Allenbrook residence, located just north of the intersection of Riverside Drive and Roswell Road (S. Atlanta Street), served as the home of the Ivy Woolen Mills superintendent. When Union troops arrived in Roswell in 1864, they found the Ivy Woolen Mills in full operation, staffed by about four hundred women. In a desperate attempt to keep the federals at bay, the Ivy Woolen Mill superintendent, Theofile Roche, had raised the French flag, in an attempt to show neutrality. The ruse was unsuccessful. The Union troops found signs that the mill was manufacturing Confederate uniforms and cloth, and the mill was burned. General Sherman ordered his commander to round up the women and their three hundred children and forced them to march on foot ten miles to Marietta. They were placed on railcars, given rations, and taken north of the Ohio River, where they were dumped. Some did not survive. Others took a long time to make it back home. This became one of the major tragedies of the war.

Today, the Roswell Mill ruins are managed more for conservation than for preservation. Other than the machinery, the dam, and the machine shop, most of the observable ruins are stone foundations. Take care not to alter or destroy these history lessons when exploring them, and be sure to watch for snakes and other hazards.

The covered bridge over Vickery Creek provides hikers with a nice introduction to the Unit's treasures.

Young hikers explore mill ruins in the Vickery Creek Unit.

Young hikers on hike number 2 in the Vickery Creek Unit.

A view of the ruins and covered bridge in the Vickery Creek Unit

The Mill Dam falls is the single most noteworthy feature in the Vickery Creek Unit.

The ruins of the mill works in the Vickery Creek Unit are always interesting.

CHAPTER 10

THE ISLAND FORD UNIT - PARK HEADQUARTERS

Directions to the Island Ford Unit

1. Take I-285 east or west to GA 400 north.
2. Go north on 400 to the North Ridge Road exit (Exit 6).
3. At the top of the ramp (which circles around), proceed to the right for 0.25 miles, and cross the bridge over GA 400.
4. After crossing the bridge, take the first right onto Dunwoody Place.
5. Proceed for less than a mile to Roberts Drive on the right.
6. Turn right onto Roberts Drive, and proceed about a mile to the entrance to the Island Ford Unit on the right.

Once you enter the unit, please note that there are three separate parking areas. The first is on the left just after you enter the unit. This parking area accesses two of the trails in this book. A second parking lot is near the fishing pond. The third parking area is at the end of the road at park headquarters. There are often bikes on the park entrance road, so be cautious.

Activities

- Picnicking
- Fishing
- Family walks

- Hiking
- Trail running
- Wildlife observation
- Boat launch
- Biking

Park headquarters provides a small store with park books and other items. Bathrooms are also located in park headquarters.

Trails

- An easy lollipop-loop walk through fine forest of about 2.5 miles (easy)
- A nice walk through woods and along the river of 1.2 to 2.4 miles (easy to moderate)
- A very easy walk around a pond suitable for little kids (easy)

Unique Sights

- Creeks
- The river
- Wildlife
- Pond
- Small waterfall
- Wildflowers

Facilities

- Pavilion for grilling and picnics
- Trails
- Trash cans
- Picnic tables
- Boat launch
- Pond
- Grills
- Park headquarters with small store and bathrooms

The Island Ford Unit is another gem of the CRNRA located upstream of the other units discussed in this book. It consists of about 297 acres, including an island in the river known as Copeland Island. The Island Ford Unit has some very nice hiking trails although none of the trails are particularly long. Some of the best fishing in the Chattahoochee River can be found alongside the Island Ford Unit. Island Ford, like Sope Creek, also contains a small pond for fishing or wildlife observation that provides a nice hike for very young children. Island Ford also has several large rock overhangs along the river that primitive men and Indians used for shelter. These outcroppings can be observed from along the river trail.

But perhaps what distinguishes the Island Ford Unit from the other units is the location of park headquarters at the end of the access road at Island Ford. The building houses administrative offices and restrooms that are open to the public. It also has a small bookstore with items relating to the Chattahoochee River and the CRNRA. The headquarters building is fascinating in and of itself. The building was constructed in the 1930s using wood from Georgia's own Okefenokee Swamp and stone from Georgia's Stone Mountain. It was the summer home of the family of Sam Hewlett, a former Georgia lawyer and superior court judge. The Hewlett family sold the property in about 1950, and the United States bought the property in 1979, at about the time of the creation of the CRNRA.

Many families go to the Island Ford Unit for picnics and fishing. Day hiking also seems to be a major activity here because the trails are short, easily accessible, and scenic. Some folks ride bikes along the park entrance road. Many of the trails along the river interconnect, so it is possible to have a varied hiking experience. The recently created Island Ford Trail is becoming more popular, but it does not connect directly to the rest of the trail system. Hikers on the Island Ford Trail can only access the remaining trails at the trailhead. But due to the scenic and peaceful nature of the trail, most hikers seem not to notice the lack of interconnections.

Trail Option 1
Island Ford Trail
(2.54-Mile Loop—Easy to Moderate)

This trail was constructed fairly recently and is just now being noticed and appreciated by hikers and trail runners. It is a lollipop loop of about

2.5 miles that showcases the forest surrounding the river and includes a short stretch of trail through the river floodplain. The woods found on this hike support populations of foxes, raccoon, beavers, muskrats, and deer. I have often seen white-tailed deer when hiking this trail and others in the Island Ford Unit. Be quiet and cautious, and hike in the early morning or at dusk, and you will have a chance to see them too.

The trail can only be easily accessed from the first parking lot in the Island Ford Unit. As you pull into the unit, look immediately to the left to spot this first parking area. Make sure that your vehicle is properly permitted for parking in the CRNRA, and start your hike at the large sign in a grassy area near the parking lot that describes the Island Ford Trail. The sign has a trail description and other information on the trail. Pass the sign on the right-hand side, and walk through a graded grassy area to a road. Cross the road (Island Ferry Road), and pick up the trail immediately on the other side.

The trail immediately enters a wooded cove and leads downhill and then around the far side of the cove through an immature forest of oaks and pines. At 0.14 miles, the trail switchbacks to the left and ascends the shoulder of a hill at 0.16 miles. At 0.24 miles, you will descend again on a series of switchbacks for about 0.1 miles. At 0.44 miles, you will cross a small draw. Go up and to the right where there is a wooden bridge over a drainage area. After this bridge, you will begin a steady descent along a drainage draw that is often dry. As you move farther and farther away from a road that parallels the trail and deeper into the woods surrounding the drainage, the sounds of the forest will begin to predominate over the sounds of civilization.

At 0.68 miles, you will reach a larger bridge over a drainage draw. If you are hiking with kids, ask the kids to make sure that there are no trolls beneath these bridges before the group crosses. After crossing this well-made bridge, you may be able to hear a small waterfall to the right, down below in the drainage. This little cascade is seasonal and may be dry during the summer months.

At 0.75 miles, you will reach the river floodplain area and begin to parallel the river downstream. The trail ascends the hillside along the river, and you may note some downed trees in this area. At 0.92 miles, you will reach two very large beech-trees and the convergence of the lollipop loop of the trail. I usually take the trail to the left to complete the loop. If you do so, you will note that the trail ascends initially deeper into the drainage. At one point, it appears to be close to the road again. However, it then begins to bend right away from the road and circle the drainage area in the small cove.

As it circles the small cove, the trail crosses small drainage draws at 1.02 miles and at 1.08 miles. At 1.19 miles, the trail begins to descend to the river bottomland, and at 1.34 miles, it makes a final, sharp switchback to the right to descend to the river floodplain area. The trail then weaves its way through the sandy floodplain to a nice overlook of the river at 1.55 miles. At 1.59 miles, there is a used short trail down to the river. Keep to the right here. At 1.62 miles, the loop portion of the trail ends at the two same large trees. Make a left, and retrace your steps back to your car at the trailhead. As you reach the trailhead, be sure to check for blackberries in the bushes surrounding the trail as it ends.

The Island Ford Trail is a nice addition to the CRNRA trail system in that it gives the hiker solitude and provides a sufficient challenge for trail runners such as myself.

Trail Option 2
River Trail
(1.25 Miles Each Way—Easy to Moderate)

This trail showcases the best of the Island Ford Unit and has enough interesting features to keep hikers entertained. It can also make a good trail run, although most trail runners would add additional mileage by running the trail two or more times or, perhaps, by running back along the park access road. There are plenty of good woods to see on this trail, but it also accesses the river, the creeks, and the remaining trail system in the unit. There are also great views of the river and rock shelters to be seen. The trail can also be used as a connector to the area near the fishing pond. I recommend this trail as a nice stroll for a family looking to have a Sunday outing. The trail is generally not sufficient for strollers or Baby Joggers, but as soon as kids are big enough to hike, they should be able to appreciate this walk.

Just as with trail option 1, this hike starts at the first parking lot nearest to the Island Ford Unit entrance. However, a hiker can also begin this hike from the headquarters building and hike the reverse direction. There are many side trails that can be utilized for loops too.

There is a signed trailhead just off the parking lot at the first parking lot. From this trailhead, the trail leads downward into the woods, at first paralleling the parking area. As with many CRNRA areas, the hardwoods along the upper reaches of this trail are beautiful, particularly in the spring and fall. At 0.1 miles, you will cross a couple of small wooden boardwalk bridges. Continue descending into the forest along the side of the ridge. At 0.19 miles, the trail skirts the hillside above a tiny spring, and shortly thereafter, the trail parallels a small creek upstream. At 0.3 miles, the trail crosses the creek at a series of pretty cascades (during wet weather) and then parallels the creek as it flows downstream. There are some impressive large oaks and pine trees to be viewed at about 0.34 miles.

At 0.4 miles, you will reach a signed trail junction. This portion of the trail has been recently rerouted by the National Park Service. If you proceed uphill in a dug-out trail leading to the right, it will lead you to the park entrance road after passing through some nice, forested areas. If you walk up the stairs from the junction and then take the branch to the right, it will lead to the river. I recommend that you walk up the stairs from the junction and then take the branch to the left, which leads downhill to the river through several switchbacks. After the switchbacks, you will parallel Beech Creek, which runs to the left of the trail, which is now a pleasant, flat, and wide path at about 0.54 miles from the trailhead. Take the time to look for fish in the creek, particularly in the section nearest to the river.

At 0.56 miles, you will reach another signed trail junction. The trail to the left goes to a loop trail near the creek. Instead, take the right fork that parallels the river upstream. Initially, you will not be near the river. However, as the hike progresses, the trail comes nearer to the river, even giving the hiker good views in some locations. At 0.63 miles, you will reach yet another signed trail junction. Taking the right-hand fork uphill will lead you back to the very first trail junction. Instead, continue to the left as the trail continues to parallel the river. At this junction, there is a very interesting rock shelter that was probably used by primitive men as shelter. Take time to inspect the rock shelter and to envision how much the rock would protect a man from a violent rainstorm. Also, one can observe from the white chalk marks on the rock that some folks have been practicing their rock climbing moves here.

Continue your walk along the river in the flat and easy floodplain. At 0.86 miles, you will reach a second rock shelter. Imagine yourself stranded here in bad weather, trying to start a fire under the rock to keep warm. At

0.89 miles from the trailhead, you will reach a third rock shelter. This one affords more protection from the elements than the previous two. At 0.94 miles, you will cross an interesting bridge over a ravine with a creek at the bottom. When the river is running high, this ravine fills with river water to nearly the top of the ditch. At 0.96 miles, you will reach another signed trail junction with a trail leading off to the right, which connects to the remainder of the trail system. There is yet another small rock shelter near this junction.

At 1.09 miles, you will reach yet another signed trail junction with a trail leading off to the right. This trail leads to the second parking lot near the fishing pond. Continue straight ahead along the riverbank. The trail is sandy and very pleasant in this area, which is nicely shaded by trees. At 1.11 miles, you will reach the high point of this hike, which is a nice metal bridge over a creek with beautiful river views. Cross the bridge. If you take a right turn after the bridge and hike upstream a few yards, you will see a very small but beautiful waterfall in the creek to your right. To your left will be a picnic pavilion and the park headquarters building. You can also hike upstream along the creek for about 0.2 miles to view some interesting features of the area.

After you cross the bridge, proceed straight ahead over some rocks and along some fencing, which provides nice views of the river. At 1.2 miles, the trail ends at some picnic tables, a boat launch, and an activity field. From here, you can take the sidewalk up to the park headquarters building, visit the bookstore, and hike back to the trailhead along the park entrance road. Alternatively, retrace your steps 1.2 miles back to the trailhead.

Trail Option 3
Short Pond Walk
(0.45 Miles—Easy)

The Island Ford Unit provides a third walk that is suitable for very young children. It circles the small fishing pond on the property and gives kids the opportunity to view small wildlife and understand ecosystems. For adults, a hike around the pond can be coupled with other portions of the unit's trail system for a longer and more extensive hike. For instance, a hike on the river trail can easily include this hike at its midpoint before a hiker returns to the trailhead at the first parking area.

To access this hike, follow the entrance road to the unit to its end in front of the main park headquarters building. Park here. Start at the signs in front of the park headquarters, and follow the sidewalk down along the left-hand side of the park headquarters building. At the sign for the Hewlett Lodge, go left and downhill on a gravel path toward the river and a small creek that flows alongside the headquarters building. At 0.05 miles, you will reach the historic picnic shelter and its picnic tables and grill at a cleared area. Continue downhill on steps until you reach the level of the creek and river. At this point, turn right, and walk a few steps to the sturdy metal bridge crossing the creek near the river. Enjoy splendid views of the river.

Next, retrace your steps back up the creek, but instead of following the path uphill to the picnic shelter area, continue to parallel the creek upstream. In a few feet, there will be an opportunity to step down to the creek level, where you will find a delightful little waterfall cascade in the creek. This is a place to be savored. After you have checked out the cascade, return to the trail, and travel upstream along the bank of the creek, which flows out of the fishing pond itself. In the spring, look for flowering daffodils and other streamside plants. If you look to the left at 0.12 miles, you will see an old well/storage house in the hillside that may be worth exploring.

At 0.17 miles, go to the right at a signed trail junction. The left-hand branch leads back to the parking lot. In a few feet, you will cross the park entrance road at a crosswalk and walk across the grass to the wooden dock on the banks of the fishing pond. If you are with kids, take time to let them explore and tell them about how pond wildlife survives. They should be able to observe frogs, turtles, and fish on this hike if they are quiet and observant. Turn to the left from the dock, and begin to circle the pond on a straightforward path. Take every opportunity to walk to the shoreline, and look for interesting plant and wildlife.

At 0.29 miles, descend some wooden stairs, and cross the pond's inlet stream on a wooden boardwalk. The lushness of this area is evident from the moist soil and plant life. This is a good place to observe frogs. Continue circling the pond. There is an interpretive sign about pond life that can be informative for younger hikers. At 0.4 miles, the trail ends at the road. A set of concrete steps leads to the left and uphill to the second parking lot. If you parked near the park headquarters, continue circling the pond, and go back across the crosswalk as you came. Instead of turning left at the trail junction, you can proceed straight ahead to your car at the parking lot. Make sure to visit the bookstore in the park headquarters building to see some fun books and materials that can enhance your next hiking experience at the CRNRA.

A bridge spans a draw along the river in the Island Ford Unit.

The first of several rock shelters encountered along the river in the Island Ford Unit.

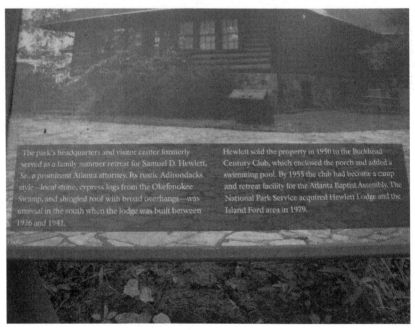

An interpretive sign describes the history of the Park Headquarters in the Island Ford Unit.

Another of the rock shelters along the river in the Island Ford Unit.

The unique Park Headquarters in the Island Ford Unit is worth a visit.

This small but beautiful cascade is one of the surprises found in the Island Ford Unit.

This unique footbridge spans a draw flowing into the river in the Island Ford Unit.

This crosswalk leads across the park entrance road to the fishing dock on the small pond.

The small pond in the Island Ford Unit is fun to explore.

This interpretive sign describes wildlife near small ponds.

This signed trailhead at the first parking lot in the Island Ford Unit leads down towards the river.

This boardwalk crosses the infeeder stream on the small pond.

NATURE/SPORTS

Wonderful Wilderness Trails Exist Minutes from Atlanta, Georgia!

Hike, bike, and trail run on trails that will remind you of the North Georgia Mountains. This is your complete trail reference for exploring the Chattahoochee River National Recreation Area on foot or by bike. This guide provides accurate trail descriptions and information that will inspire you to explore. You will want to take this book along on your hike.

This book will allow you to discover the following:

- Natural beauty that you never thought existed so close to Atlanta
- Sparsely traveled trails close to the Atlanta area that will make you wonder whether you have wandered into a much larger mountainous wilderness
- Interesting historical sites and other features, many of which are known to very few people
- Great places to test your trail-running skills and to train for longer runs
- Trails that will challenge your mountain biking skills
- Hidden pockets of nature that few other folks enjoy
- Amazing animals and plants that live close to the metropolitan Atlanta area
- What to expect and what to bring on a hike, run, or bike ride in the Chattahoochee River National Recreation Area

William Linkous has been a resident of the North Atlanta area for nearly fifty years. William grew up only a couple of miles from the Chattahoochee River National Recreation Area and many of the areas described in this book. He spent much of his childhood exploring the area and has been a regular visitor to the CRNRA during most of his adult life. He has spent countless hours hiking, trail running, biking, rock climbing, paddling, and fishing in the CRNRA. William is also a photographer, who has contributed his prints to the CRNRA.

This trail guide will help you find and explore CRNRA trails that you never knew existed. A wilderness adventure awaits you!

INDEX

A

access point, 22–23, 50, 73, 85–86
Akers Mill, 20, 23, 25, 32
Akers Mill Drive, 20, 22, 27, 31
Akers Mill Road, 26–27, 32
Allenbrook, 165–67, 174
animals, 6–7, 10, 15, 17–18, 50, 53, 84–85, 92, 125, 146–47, 149, 165–66, 171–72, 195
anoles, 7, 52, 136
Arrowhead Creek, 133
Atlanta, ix, xi, 1, 6, 10, 14, 17–18, 22–23, 27, 32, 55, 84–85, 101–2, 150–51, 195
Atlanta Water and Electric Power Company, 146, 151

B

Baby Joggers, 3, 9, 16, 84–85, 89, 183
backcountry, 16–18
Balcony, 93, 96–97, 99, 101–2
bathrooms, 22, 31–32, 83, 85, 87–88, 180
beavers, ix, 5, 7, 15, 24, 50, 84, 86–90, 92, 146, 149, 152, 182
Beech Creek, 184
bees, 16
bikers, x, 12, 27, 82, 88, 92, 94, 97, 100–102, 119, 127
bikes, x, 2, 4, 9–10, 12–13, 17, 22–24, 50, 85, 87–89, 92–97, 99–101, 103, 127, 195
biking, ix–x, 2, 4, 10, 12–13, 23, 25–26, 82–85, 88, 92–94, 96–101, 103, 127, 133–34, 195
birds, 5–7, 14–15, 23, 50, 53, 73, 75, 89, 91–92, 97, 102, 107, 125–26, 146
boating, 5
Bob Callan Trail, 23, 26
bookstore, 185–86
Brevard Fault, 49–50, 54
bridge, Akers Mill Road, 26
bridges
    metal, 51–53
    Rottenwood Creek, 24, 28–32
    wooden, 51, 56–57, 59, 99, 103, 148, 152, 182
Bull Sluice Lake, vii, 5, 7, 145–48, 151–52, 156

C

canoes, 5, 22, 73
Charlie's Trapping Creek, 51–52

Chattahoochee River, vii, ix, xi, 5, 19, 24, 27, 34, 49, 57, 74, 76, 117, 181, 195
children, 3, 6, 9, 102, 106, 174, 181, 185
Civil War, 103, 172–74
cliffs, 17, 21, 29–31, 33, 51, 57, 59–60, 167
Cochran Shoals Unit, ix–x, xii, 4, 7, 9, 11, 16, 26–27, 72, 80, 83–86, 94–95, 98, 103–5, 112–15
Columns Drive, x, 4, 27, 81–83, 85–88, 107, 124–25, 127, 132–34
conservation, 18, 174
Copeland Island, 181
copperheads, 7, 16
coyotes, ix, 7, 10, 15, 84, 96
creeks, 6, 23–26, 32, 42–43, 55–58, 88–93, 95, 98–99, 104–7, 133, 135–36, 146–48, 165–68, 170–73, 183–86
CRNRA (Chattahoochee River National Recreation Area), vii–xii, 1–18, 20, 34, 55, 83, 89–93, 95–96, 101–3, 105, 125–26, 136–37, 168–69, 181–84, 195

D

dams, 90, 102, 116, 146, 151, 165–66, 170–71, 173–74
dangers, 5, 8–9
deer, ix, 7, 10, 15, 50, 84, 87–88, 126, 135, 146, 165–66, 171, 182
Devil's Racecourse Shoals, 31, 49–50
dogs, x, 12, 18, 23
ducks, 27, 29, 73, 89–90, 146

E

East Palisades Unit, 49–50, 58, 60–70

entrance, 20, 28, 47, 51, 55, 63, 86–87, 89, 92–93, 98–99, 107–8, 110, 144, 163–64, 166–67
erosion, 4, 12, 18, 56, 83, 91, 99, 101
exploration, 5, 72, 92, 104, 126, 167, 169, 171, 173

F

facilities, 2, 9, 22, 49–50, 72, 77, 83, 125, 133, 145, 165, 180
fall, ix, xi, 6, 8–11, 13, 17, 24, 27–28, 32, 49, 53–56, 75, 84–85, 87–91, 133–35
families, vii, x, 3, 8–9, 21–22, 28, 48, 54, 71, 81, 84–85, 96, 102–3, 124, 181
fields, activity, 22, 24, 87, 145, 185
fish, 6, 9, 50, 52–53, 57–58, 87–88, 95, 102–3, 107, 136, 184, 186
  bass, 5–6, 51, 57, 102, 135
  bream, 5–6, 51, 57, 102
  trout, 5–6, 53, 89, 151
fishermen, 6, 12, 22–23, 89, 145, 148
fishing, vii, 2, 5–6, 21, 23, 26, 32, 58, 84–85, 102–3, 144–45, 147–48, 179, 181, 185–86
floodplains, 22, 28, 49–50, 74, 76–77, 86, 88, 90, 95, 97, 125, 182
flowers, 9, 18, 55, 85, 89–91, 99, 127, 132–35, 137, 167
fly-fishing, 5
food, 13–14, 53
forest, 28–29, 48–50, 53–57, 74, 76–78, 88–89, 91–93, 96, 98–99, 103–4, 135–36, 150–52, 169, 171, 182
Fox Creek, 99, 101
foxes, 7, 50, 84, 126, 165, 182
frogs, 76, 89–90, 97, 135, 186

G

Garrard, Kenner, 105
gear, 5–6, 13–14
geese, Canadian, 6, 73, 75–76, 84, 149
Georgia, 3, 6, 30, 49, 171, 173, 181, 195
Gold Branch Unit, 5, 144–47, 149–50, 154–62
Grimes Bridge Road, 171
Gumby Creek, 89, 91–92

H

Harris Trail, 47
hawks, ix, 7, 14–15, 84, 125, 135, 146, 165–66
hazards, 3, 15, 17, 174
herons, ix, 6–7, 10, 14, 29, 73, 75, 84, 87, 146
Hewlett, Sam, 181
hikers, 2, 6–7, 10–14, 25–28, 31, 49–50, 82–83, 98–99, 101–5, 127, 145–46, 151–52, 168–69, 181, 183–85
  average-to-slow, 98
  casual, 126–27
  intrepid, 82
  observant, 7, 133
  overnight, 13
  winter, 10
  younger, 186
  youthful, 9
hikes
  day, 13–14, 167, 181
  evening, 10, 166
  lollipop-loop, 48, 52, 89
  out-and-back, 21, 48, 55, 72
  short, 13, 51, 126, 134
  short-loop, 28

hiking, vii, 2–3, 13–18, 21–23, 26, 31–32, 72, 74, 83–84, 91, 124–26, 144–47, 164–66, 170–71, 180–82
  easy, 23, 171
  remotest, 170
hiking stores, 13
hills, ix, 10, 26, 28, 32, 51, 53, 75, 81, 84, 88–89, 91, 94–96, 99, 167
  rolling, 146, 148
  steep, 23
hillsides, 25–26, 51, 53, 55–56, 74–76, 104, 135, 148–50, 167, 182, 184, 186
hilltops, 172
homesites, 75–76, 169
homesteads, 25, 48, 50, 55, 57, 59, 82–83, 100, 169
hummingbirds, 89–90

I

Indian Trail Road, 47–48, 50, 54–55, 59
injury, 15, 17, 173
  causes of, 17
  lightning, 17
  serious, 17
  terrible, 17
insects, 17, 171
Interstate North Parkway, 71, 80, 86, 89
Island Ferry Road, 182
Island Ford Trail, 181–83
Island Ford Unit, 1–2, 4–5, 7, 11, 76, 179, 181–83, 185
islands, 73, 149, 181
Ivy Woolen Mill, 165–66, 173–74

J

Johnson, William, 125
Johnson's Ferry North Unit, 5, 7, 132–33

Johnson's Ferry Road, 81, 88, 124, 132, 144
Johnson's Ferry South Unit, 8, 124–27, 136–37

K

kayakers, 5, 87, 149
kayaks, 73
kids, 9, 14, 23, 52–54, 56, 58, 85, 102–3, 134, 167, 180, 182–83, 185–86
King, Barrington, 173
King, Roswell, 173

L

lake, 5, 16, 145–46, 148–50, 152
lakeshore, 145, 147–52
Lanier, Lake, 5
litter, 12
  dog, 12
lizards, 7, 50, 89–90, 125
Long Island Creek, 9, 49–53, 57, 64
Long Island Shoals, 29, 49, 51
loops, 3, 28, 30, 32, 48, 53, 74, 77, 86–88, 97–98, 101–3, 133–35, 147, 150–51, 182–83
  fitness-trail, 92
  lollipop, 84, 86–88, 136, 169–70, 181–82
  moderate-trail, 94
  mountain bike, 87, 94
  mountain biking, 92–94, 97
  pond, 102–3
  short, 30–32, 82, 94

M

manholes, 24, 93
maps, x, 2, 15, 28

National Park Service, 2
Marietta Paper Mill, 82, 103
mills, ix, 25, 103, 105, 173–74
Mill Street, 163–64, 166–68, 170, 172–73
Morgan Falls Dam, 5, 145–46, 151
Morgan Falls Road, 151
mountain laurel, 9, 21, 30–31, 49, 53–56, 100, 148
mountains, xi, 3, 11, 28, 72
Mount Paran Road, 47
Mulberry Creek, 133–34, 136
muscadine vines, 169
muskrats, 7, 84, 182

N

Nannyberry Creek, 133–34
National Park Service, xi, 2, 4, 11–12, 16, 18, 56, 59, 73–74, 83, 91–93, 99, 101, 125–27, 184
New Northside Drive, 20, 32, 47, 71, 80
North Georgia Mountains, 22, 25, 30, 54, 91, 195
Northridge Road, 163
Northside Drive, 20–21, 47–48, 71, 80

O

opossums, 7, 15, 146
Owl Creek, 133
owls, ix, 6–7, 10, 14, 84, 125, 135, 146, 165–66, 171–72
  barred, 7, 84, 97, 166, 171–72
Oxbo Road, 164, 170, 172

P

Paces Mill, 5, 11, 22–23, 33
paddling, vii, ix–x, 3, 5, 32, 145, 195
  flat-water, 5

Paper Mill Road, 81, 104–5
park headquarters, 179–81, 185–86, 189
parking, 10–11, 22, 26, 47–48, 54–55, 59, 71–72, 80–81, 88, 126, 163–64, 166–68, 179, 182, 184–85
  overflow, 72
parking lot, 4, 27, 55–56, 72, 74, 76–77, 84, 86–88, 94–95, 98, 126–27, 134, 150, 170, 182–86
pavilions, 8, 72, 125, 132–33, 180
photography, nature, 15
Picnicking, 2, 8–9, 21, 48, 71, 81, 124, 132, 144, 164, 179
picnics, 8, 180–81
picnic tables, 8, 22, 49–50, 72, 83, 85–86, 102, 104, 133, 145, 147, 165, 172, 180, 185–86
ponds, 4, 6–7, 28, 82, 91–92, 94, 100–104, 135, 179–81, 183, 185–86
  beaver, 6, 16
  CRNRA, 9
  fishing, 179, 183, 185–86
    small, 185
  small, 6, 181, 191–92, 194
  wildlife, 91–92
Power, James, 74
Powers Ferry Road, 20–21, 32, 47, 71, 80
Powers Island Unit, 5, 7–8, 11, 22, 71–74, 80, 86, 146

R

rabbits, 7–8, 10, 125–26, 146
raccoon, 7, 10, 15, 146, 182
rafts, 5, 22, 49–51, 72–73
  inflatable, 32–33
ravines, 26, 185
regulations, x, 5–6, 11–12, 103, 127, 169
rhododendron, 9, 30–31

riverbanks, 51, 53, 57, 59, 72, 74, 126, 129, 136, 185
Riverside Drive, 81, 124, 132, 144, 166–67, 174
Roberts Drive, 179
Roche, Theofile, 174
Rock Climbing, vii, x, 3, 8, 33–34, 184, 195
rock shelter, 48–49, 51–53, 82, 145, 147–49, 184–85
Roswell Manufacturing Company, 165–66, 172–73
Roswell Mill, 165, 174
Roswell Road, 144, 151, 163–64, 166, 174
Rottenwood Creek, 23–24, 29, 32
Rottenwood Creek Multiuse Trail, 21–24, 26–30
routes
  main hiking, 74
  possible biking/running, 23
  trail-running, 106
ruins, 23–25, 32, 48, 55, 57, 75, 82, 104–5, 115, 165–66, 172–73, 177–78
  historical, 23, 82–84, 104
  mill, ix, 25, 105, 107, 164, 176
rules, x, 6, 11–12, 18
  conservation, 18
runners, ix–x, 3, 6, 13, 16, 26–27, 29, 85, 119, 127
  trail, 14, 22, 89, 94, 105–6, 181, 183
running, trail, ix, 3–4, 7, 10, 14, 17, 25, 29, 83–84, 88, 94, 98, 105–6, 145–47, 195
  long-distance, 14

S

safety, 1, 8, 13, 15, 34
salamanders, 7, 84, 90, 97, 172
seasons, ix, 10, 99
  wet, 88, 90, 135
shoals, 29, 49–51, 54, 67
shorelines, 102–3, 186
Sibley Creek, 87–88, 93, 95, 98, 101
Sibley Pond, xv–xvi, 4, 82, 92, 94, 100–104, 116
sidebars, 32–33, 57–58, 105–6, 127, 136, 172
sidewalks, 170, 172, 185–86
signs, trail, 28–32, 51, 74, 93, 141, 168
snakes, 7, 15–16, 25, 84, 88, 125, 135–36, 174
  banded water, 7, 15–16, 84
  black rat, 7, 15, 84, 97
  nonpoisonous, 15–16
  ring-necked, 7, 15–16
  water, 15, 136
solitude, xi, 41, 49, 52, 55, 72, 80, 84, 91, 101, 133, 145, 165–66
Sope Creek Unit, x, 4, 6–7, 9, 25, 81–82, 94, 96, 98, 100, 102–7, 116–17, 119–20, 122–23, 137
spiders, 17
spring, ix, 6–11, 13–14, 23–24, 53–56, 58, 74–77, 84–85, 89–93, 95–96, 98–99, 126–27, 132–36, 146–47, 166–67
strolls, 53, 55, 87, 102
  casual, 74, 82
  one-mile forest, 21, 27
summer, ix, 6, 8–11, 13–14, 17, 23–24, 49, 51–52, 58, 76, 84–85, 87–88, 91, 165–66, 181–82

switchbacks, 12, 18, 27, 56, 99, 101, 147, 150, 167, 182, 184

T

temperature, 10, 14, 27
Thornton Shoals, 31, 49
thunderstorms, 10, 14, 17, 76
toads, 23–24, 84, 89–90, 97
trailheads
  Cochran Shoals, 101
  Highway 41, 24–25
  Indian Trail Road, 54–55, 59
  Interstate North Parkway, 89
  Oxbo, 164
  Paces Mill, 22
  signed, 56, 91–92, 184
  Sope Creek Unit, 102, 104
  Whitewater Creek, 49–53
trail intersections, signed, 51, 53, 56, 96, 148
trails, ix–xi, 2–4, 12–18, 21–33, 47–48, 50–57, 59, 72–77, 82–106, 125–27, 134–37, 145–53, 166–73, 181–86, 195
  blue-blazed, 54, 148–50, 168
  dirt, 168–69, 171
  fitness, ix–x, 4, 7, 9, 16, 82–89, 91–96, 98, 101–2, 108–12
  flat, 102, 150
  hiking, vii, 22, 83, 103
  interpretive, 166, 173
  lakeshore, 146–47, 150, 152
    easy, 147
  loop, 29–31, 74–77, 101, 103, 134–35, 150, 171, 184
  maintained, 2, 12, 148
  marked, 2, 12, 27, 53
  mountain bike, 95–97, 99–100, 114

mountain biking, x, 4, 92, 94, 96–101, 103
multiuse, 22–31
narrow, 135, 169, 171
nice, 100–101, 168
open, 2, 12
paved, 23–24, 28
remote, 3, 17, 83–84
return, 151, 169
river, 181, 183, 185
short, 85, 87, 166
side, 96, 99, 101, 135, 183
signed, 75, 101, 168
unmarked, 2, 53
used, 12, 53–54, 146–49, 167, 169, 171
user, 51, 56
wide, 30, 102, 131, 134, 171
trail system, 24, 28, 50, 74, 83, 86–88, 96, 138, 164, 166, 171, 181, 183, 185
  mountain biking, 82, 94, 99
  upper, 88
trash, x, 12, 18, 49–50, 55, 125
trees, ix, xi, 10–11, 17, 26–28, 50–51, 55, 75–76, 86–87, 90–92, 100–101, 151, 168–69, 171, 182–85
  downed, 67, 151, 159, 171, 182
  large, 87, 183
  oak, 96, 169
  pine, 24, 91, 100, 152, 184
trellis, 164, 168, 170
trillium, 9
  catesby's, 9, 85, 90, 99, 134, 137
  toadshade, 9, 85, 90, 99, 134, 136–37
tunnels, 96, 151
turnoffs, 27, 96–98
turtles, xvi, 7, 16, 23–24, 57, 84, 87, 90, 97, 103, 135, 186

  eastern box, 7
  musk, 7
  painted, 7, 23, 84
  snapping, 7, 16, 57, 84

V

Vickery Creek Unit, 163, 165–70, 172–73, 176–78

W

Waller Park, 164, 166, 170–72
water, vii, ix, 5–7, 14–17, 33, 51, 53–54, 57–58, 84, 86–91, 105–6, 133, 136, 148–49, 151–52
watercraft, 49, 73
waterfalls, 173
  small, 82, 180, 182
waterfowl, 23–24, 29, 73
weather, 10, 86, 88–89, 126, 146–47, 149, 152, 172, 184
West Palisades Unit, 8–9, 27, 29, 34–38, 50, 67, 73
Whitewater Creek Road, 47, 50
wilderness, 26, 85, 99, 101
wildflowers, ix, 9–11, 24, 75, 77, 82, 84, 87, 89, 91, 102, 113, 133–34, 145–46, 165–66
  spring, 11
  viewing, 9
wildlife, ix, 5–6, 8, 22–23, 73, 83–84, 86–87, 90–92, 97–98, 124–26, 145–47, 164–68, 170–71, 180–81, 185–86
  pond, 186
  viewing, 8, 73, 83
wildlife observation, 2, 6, 21, 48, 72, 81, 124, 132, 144, 147, 164, 180–81

winter, ix, 8, 10–11, 13–14, 27, 30, 51, 54, 75, 84, 86, 88, 91, 101–2, 167
woodpeckers, 7, 100, 146
  pileated, 84, 97
  redheaded, 73
woods, x, 2, 4, 7, 11, 15, 22, 27, 52, 75, 82–84, 96–106, 126, 146–51, 180–82
  deep, 3, 17, 98
  upland, 30, 149
  upper, 76

Made in the USA
Lexington, KY
03 December 2017